Also available at all good book stores

9781785310126

9781785314902

9781785315510

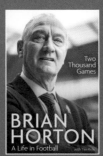

9781785316685

9781785316807

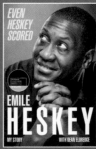

9781785315008

9781785316333

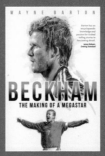

9781785316760

9781785314995

THE 'LIMPING' PHYSIO

THE
'LIMPING'
PHYSIO

JOHN SHERIDAN
A Life in Football

Forewords by
**David Pleat &
Gary Mabbutt MBE**

First published by Pitch Publishing, 2021

Pitch Publishing
A2 Yeoman Gate
Yeoman Way
Worthing
Sussex
BN13 3QZ
www.pitchpublishing.co.uk
info@pitchpublishing.co.uk

A CIP catalogue record is available for this book
from the British Library.

ISBN 978 1 80150 007 4

Typesetting and origination by Pitch Publishing
Printed and bound in India by Replika Press Pvt. Ltd.

Contents

Foreword by David Pleat 7

Foreword by Gary Mabbutt MBE 9

Preface 11

1. My Early Years .13

2. From Production Line to Professional Football 27

3. In at the Deep End 43

4. Surgeons, Injuries and Professor Smillie 53

5. Life at Luton in the 1980s 68

6. Off to Spurs 87

7. All Change at Spurs 97

8. Paul Gascoigne and that Free Kick 107

9. That Tackle 116

10. The Fightback Begins and Fishy Tales 123

11. Disaster and the Fightback Begins Again 135

12. The Beginning of the End at Tottenham 148

13. A New Start 159

14. Stories from Around the World 168

15. Matchdays 180

16. Injury Management, Assessment and Rehabilitation . . 188

17. Other Memories 206

18. Fun on the Fairway 221

19. Looking Back 229

Postscript 235

Acknowledgements 250

Foreword by David Pleat

DURING MY lengthy career in football I have come across many physios at both youth and senior level. John Sheridan is unique!

I employed him at Luton Town shortly after I took over in 1979. John had been recommended to me by an employee who knew him from his role as safety officer at Whitbread's. I got lucky! He was a hard worker who would spend whatever hours were required – never a free Sunday. More importantly we soon realised he had a magic touch and the players respected him for his commitment and understanding of their problems. He became a vital member of our staff – the health and welfare of our players was paramount.

John studied hard and learnt the intricacies of the physiotherapy business, and gained his reward when he became a fully chartered physiotherapist. Players respected him for his attention to detail and ability to progress their injury to full fitness. Nothing was too much trouble.

When a player was felled by injury on the field, John would anticipate with his eagle eye and race on, all the more remarkable because John himself had incurred a limp as a consequence of an accident in his younger days. Some ignorant observers thought it did not look good that the guy treating the injury was injured himself! This disability never troubled John and certainly never concerned me as manager. I knew everyone who worked with him had total respect for him and his ability to perform his job. Bobby Robson once remarked to me that you must have courage to employ a physio who can't run. I replied that it is he who has the courage, for he is a special man.

When I left for Tottenham, I had no second thoughts when I invited John to join me. There he continued to treat players at the top of the footballing tree – established internationals were handled with care. The famous Paul Gascoigne was nursed back to fitness after a bad injury and John went to Lazio with him to help with his recovery.

I hope this book gives you an insight into this special man. A dedicated, kind, knowledgeable and respected person, who over the years many footballers had reason to thank.

David Pleat, January 2021

Foreword by Gary Mabbutt MBE

DURING THE seven years that John Sheridan spent at Spurs, I did not hear anyone have a bad word to say about him. He was an excellent physiotherapist and a gentleman.

In his role as a physio, John was always more concerned with the individual's health and fitness rather than declaring a player fit to play before he was 100 per cent ready.

Personally, me being physically fit to play was also dependent on my type one diabetes being looked after. I was on four injections a day during my career at Spurs and on ten blood tests a day to check my blood sugar levels.

Throughout my career this was all managed by myself but with the backup of a great medical team behind me, and John was always covering my back should any complications arise.

I trusted John 100 per cent. His knowledge of his profession and his expertise were all tested to the utmost degree when being involved in professional football and he carried out his role with great aplomb.

I was once asked the question about whether John's disability had affected his duties and I was bewildered. I had never once even considered that John had a disability. Yes, he had a limp but not once did this ever affect his ability to fulfil his role.

John was a pleasure to work with during his time at Tottenham Hotspur FC.

Gary Mabbutt, January 2021

Preface

WHEN I first sat down to write this book it was primarily for my four beloved grandchildren – Jake, Sam, Lucy and Edward. They would often ask me about my career and time in football, so I decided it was about time to put pen to paper, write down a few of my memories and see where it took me. It was a slow start but the more I wrote the more the recollections, both good and bad, came flooding back. I soon realised that I have had a great life experiencing the highs and lows, with the joys and tears of non-league football through to the professional game at the highest level.

To be able to enjoy a long and successful career in any professional sport you have to make sacrifices and have the support of a loving family, which I am lucky to have. My wife Betty has always been my backbone. She has given me all of her love and support, and looking back I now realise that I have sometimes taken her for granted by spending long hours away from her and my children Debbie, Andy and Paul. I have lost count of the amount of times I had to rush off after hurriedly eating a Christmas dinner and not return until late on Boxing Day evening, then be back up bright and early the next morning to go to the ground and treat the injured players in preparation for the New Year's Day matches.

My story in football stretches over five decades, with literally thousands of games and in fact over 1,000 at the highest level. To have achieved this, I have to thank all of the managers and staff I have worked for and of course a big thank you goes to all of the players I have treated over the years, from the local park players to some of the world's greatest icons of the game. Looking back, I can honestly say I gave each and every one of them 100 per cent.

I would also like to thank my youngest son Paul for putting my notes and ramblings into some sort of order. I am indebted to him for all the hours and hours he has spent deciphering my memories from the scraps of paper I gave him. I am sure he has enjoyed it and along the way learnt a few things about his old dad that he never knew before!

This book is about a boy born in Glasgow who suffered life-changing injuries as a teenager but through the love, care and support of his family rebuilt his life to enjoy a long and successful career in elite sport. It is a book that has come from the heart and even though it hasn't been professionally written, I hope it gives you an interesting insight into my life.

If you pick up this book, I hope you enjoy reading it as much as I have enjoyed reliving the memories of my life. John xxxx

1

My Early Years

WHAT I want to do in this book is to tell the story of my life to share with my family and friends. It has been an astonishing journey with many highs and lows, and I have been lucky enough to meet some wonderful people along the way and have made some fantastic lifelong friends. From humble beginnings working as a trainer for Taverners to travelling the world and going to some of the greatest football stadiums as a physiotherapist with Luton Town and Tottenham Hotspur, it has been a pleasure and privilege every step of the way.

Let me start from the beginning. I was born during the Second World War in Glasgow in February 1943. At the time, my father Thomas was serving in the Highland Light Infantry as a chef and was posted to Africa. While he was away our home was Maryhill Barracks in Glasgow. Dad was a brave man who like many of his peers very rarely spoke about the war. In fact, I can only remember one occasion when he spoke to me about his experiences of that time. We had gone for a drink together at the Shepherd and Flock pub in Luton, when he started to get emotional as he told me some of his memories including the landing in Africa and losing some of his friends.

After the war had finished, Dad returned home. He had to look for a job and it was decided we would move south to

England as there were many more job opportunities. So just after I turned three, my dad, mum Edna and my two older brothers Tony and Tommy moved to Luton in Bedfordshire. Our first house in the town was 38 Abbey Drive, a newly built semi-detached three-bedroom council house. Luton was a good place to live at the time – a thriving market town with a vast workforce and numerous job opportunities at large companies such as Vauxhall Motors, Electrolux and SKF. There was a big open market and numerous shops, which was the heart of the town up until the early 1970s when they were unfortunately demolished for the new Arndale Shopping Centre.

Not long after we arrived, Dad found employment at Vauxhall as a press tool operator. We settled quickly, so much so that our family increased during this time as my beloved sisters Anne and Pat were born. We were a working-class family. Dad worked long hours and Mum had various cleaning jobs just to make ends meet but my childhood was an extremely happy one.

Although we didn't have a lot of money, Mum and Dad would always try and take us on holiday during the summer. We would go from Luton to Rye, in East Sussex, to stay with my step-grandma Annie and grandad Tommy at their pub, the Plough Inn. Mum and Dad would be there for a week before heading back to Luton while us children would remain there for the rest of the summer break. It was more of a working holiday as Grandma and Grandad trained me to work in their pub. So, from 12 years old I could clean the pipes, change the barrels and sometimes run the bar when Grandad was having a break. I was told that some customers would come in for a drink just to get served by this young barman!

We also had more family in Rye as my mum's sister lived locally, so sometimes I would go and stay with Auntie Jean and Uncle Tim. Uncle Tim was an extremely clever man and I quickly formed a strong bond with him. He showed me how to fish in the many rivers nearby and taught me how to enjoy living in the country; we would spend many hours roaming the Sussex countryside. He told me I was like a second son to him, right up until the day he passed away.

As our family was growing bigger my eldest brother Tommy went to live with Grandma and Grandad in Rye. He was extremely talented as a child and became head boy at Rye Grammar School before joining the RAF, where he was a telecommunications engineer and served in the Cypriot War of Independence between 1955 until 1959. I was always very close to Tommy, who was a great brother and would always look after me. Whenever he came back for a visit he would take me to watch a football match at either Luton Town or Leicester City. My other brother Tony went into the army and served in the Malayan Emergency until he demobbed in 1960 and joined the local police force in Luton.

My first school was Hart Hill Infant and Juniors. I was academically average but like most boys of that age I just wanted to be outside playing sport. When it was time to leave the juniors, I went to Old Bedford Road Senior School. It had a reputation for being a tough place to go to but I have good memories of this period of my life until my education was cruelly cut short.

On a cold, damp winter's day in 1957, I had an accident which would change my life forever. My dear mother had scrimped and scraped for a long time to save money for my birthday present. Not long after my birthday I was happily riding my bike when disaster struck. I had just cycled through Abbotswood Field, but the tyres must have picked up some mud because as soon as I got back on to the road my back wheel slid from under me. I lost my balance and fell off on to my left hip on the rock-hard road. After managing to get up, I still felt shocked but dusted myself down and limped home with wounded pride. Over the next few days I began to feel unwell and the pain in my hip gradually got worse, until I woke up in bed one morning with a high temperature. As soon as Mum saw me she knew that something was seriously wrong. I remember her dropping everything and rushing me to A&E at the Luton and Dunstable Hospital. As soon as the doctor examined me, I was immediately admitted to the ward and was then seen by an orthopaedic consultant.

My condition quickly deteriorated and I was transferred to the intensive care unit. To help get my high temperature under control, the nurses used ice packs and surrounded my bed with fans. Unfortunately, over the next few weeks, I became gravely ill and was fighting for my life. At one point my brother Tommy, who was serving in Cyprus in the RAF, was flown home as I wasn't expected to make it through the night. I continued to fight and with the help of penicillin I gradually recovered. My stay in hospital lasted for four months and tests showed that I had developed osteomyelitis in my left femur, which is a serious bacterial infection that spreads to the bone.

After finally leaving hospital I was allowed to go back to school. However, a few months later disaster struck again. As my hip was still weak, I had to get the bus to and from school. One lunchtime I was travelling home and the bus I was on approached my stop so I got up from my seat on the top deck. As I started to walk down the steep stairs I tripped and fell all the way down to the bottom, ending up on the platform of the bus. I managed to crawl off the platform and ended up sprawled on the pavement in extreme pain. Unbeknown to me

I had sustained a triple fracture of the same left femur that I had just recovered from.

Somehow I got up on to my feet and with all my weight on my right leg I started to hop home. I had to hang on to fences and lampposts to keep my balance. If things couldn't get any worse, as I approached home, I fell over the wall into our front garden. I can't remember getting into the house but when Mum came home from work, she found me unconscious on the dining room floor. An ambulance was called and I was rushed to Luton and Dunstable Hospital where they managed to stabilise my condition. However, due to the severity of my injury I was transferred to the Royal National Orthopaedic Hospital in Stanmore for further assessment and the treatment that would hopefully get me back to a normal life. I certainly owe the hospital so much for how I was treated in those early days.

It was one of the leading orthopaedic hospitals in the country. Throughout my time there I was in a ward with boys of a similar age. The majority were long-term patients, with many suffering from polio. While I was there I made some good friends. I remember one occasion when myself and another lad almost got into trouble with the police. After a long time spent in bed, I had finally been able to get up with the aid of crutches, so the two of us decided to get some fresh air and explore our surroundings. We found a hole in the fence and somehow managed to get through to the other side, where we then found ourselves on the property of the London Transport Sports Club. The building was unlocked and we both hobbled on our crutches into the sports hall. Inside we found some archery equipment, so there was nothing else for it and we enjoyed a couple of hours of archery practice. It seems as if we didn't tidy up well enough as a couple of days later the police visited the hospital investigating a break-in at the sports club. We pleaded our innocence, saying, 'It couldn't have been us, there is no way we could have broken in on crutches.' Our pleas seemed to work but that was the end of our archery escapades!

Without fail my dear mum would come and see me every weekend, even though back in those days it was a long and arduous journey. She would have to catch three buses from Luton to Stanmore then three buses back again, which must have taken her all day. I have always had a passion for seafood, so the day before a visit she would make a special trip to the market to buy me some cockles and whelks, and if I was really lucky Mum would occasionally bring a pot of jellied eels. I bet the other people on the bus loved the strong smell of fish every week.

The hospital staff were great, and sometimes they would arrange entertainment for us to improve morale. I remember on one occasion the famous pianist Russ Conway treated us to a performance of his new number one hit, 'Side Saddle', but unfortunately I was unable to get up and dance.

I spent about 14 months there trying to recover. The treatment consisted of traction, plaster and physiotherapy. Even after all this help, my left leg had become approximately four inches shorter than my right leg, which was due to the growth plate being damaged in my left femur. Near the end of my stay in hospital I remember the nursing staff telling me, 'Unfortunately you will never walk without aid ever again.'

Throughout this long period my schooling had suffered badly. Even though they provided two part-time teachers I hadn't really learnt a lot during that time. I had gone from being a young lad who loved sport to being a lad who couldn't walk without sticks. Before my injury I had a bubbly personality but the couple of years of pain and treatment had taken its toll on me. I became introverted and was worried if I would ever find work. I was a young man in the prime of life but with a disability and had to use two walking sticks and a modified shoe to walk.

Despite everything I had been through, I was determined to lead as normal a life as possible. Just before my 16th birthday I decided to go to the Labour Exchange to try and find a job. There were plenty of opportunities and one of the first ones I came across was for a French polisher. To be honest I didn't even know what the job entailed but undeterred, I went for an interview and was offered the position. My first job was as a trainee French polisher at Blundell's Furniture Workshop in Castle Street, Luton, under the excellent tuition of John George.

Getting out into the real world was a godsend and helped me regain some degree of confidence and normality. Since coming out of hospital I had managed to get rid of one of the two sticks that I needed to walk, but I still relied heavily on that remaining aid. While working on the furniture I would leave the stick hanging safely on a coat hook in the polishing room. After about three months in the job I had just finished a long day then tidied up and put the tools away. Just before putting my coat on I went to get to my stick, which was nowhere to be seen. I looked at John George and discovered he had sawn it in half. John was a good man who looked after me when I first started at Blundell's, but he thought I could walk unaided so in his wisdom he decided to destroy my stick. At the time I remember feeling devastated as I had accepted I would need a stick and felt unable to walk without it. I managed to limp to the bus stop and make it home. John was right – the loss of having a stick was a blessing in disguise as I slowly learned to walk without it.

However, even though I had managed to get rid of the sticks I was still having problems with my leg and the modified shoe I wore. To help me walk I would visit a cobbler in Castle Street to adapt all of my left shoes. He would put a four-inch sole on them but I would continually wear them down. So, when I was about 22, I went to see my consultant and asked about the possibility of shortening my right leg to match my left. He tried to dissuade me from having it done as it was a big and risky operation. But with great reluctance he agreed to perform an osteotomy, which consisted of cutting my right femur and removing part of it, realigning it then plating the bone to encourage it to heal. Although there was a risk, my mum knew how important this operation was to me – she gave me her blessing as she just wanted me to be happy. The operation was a success, so after four weeks in hospital, I walked out on crutches having gone from 6ft 1in to 5ft 9in tall but importantly my limp wasn't as pronounced. I couldn't wait to get home so I could throw away all of my modified shoes and go shopping for trousers of the same leg length. I am paying for it now though as whenever I go to the doctors and my BMI is checked I have to tell them that I used to be 6ft 1in and that I haven't been over-eating!

With my new-found confidence and zest for life, I regained some much-needed independence and enjoyed a social life. I had a good group of friends, and we would go to the Monkey Puzzle Club in Round Green to play snooker or enjoy watching the cream of the best 1960s groups at the Majestic Dance Hall. My confidence had grown so much that I even worked as a barman in the Jolly Topers pub in Round Green.

I also decided it was time to get more mobile so I bought a moped. After riding on a provisional licence for approximately six months it was time to get a bigger bike. However, gaining my motorcycle licence wasn't as plain-sailing as I had hoped in the era when the examiner would say, 'Off you go, son. I will walk around and watch from the pavement.' I set off confidently, noticing the examiner at various points of the route, and things were seemingly going well – then disaster, as I rode on a busy road near the town hall and a pedestrian stepped off the kerb into my path. It was too late to swerve out of the way so I hit him with a loud 'THUD'. He went flying and somehow I managed to stay on my bike, but unfortunately the examiner witnessed the whole episode. I returned to the test centre fearing the worst, and my fears then became reality when the examiner turned to me and said, 'I'm afraid you have failed, Mr Sheridan. The reason is because you hit a pedestrian, which is a shame as you were doing well.' I was disappointed but understood, so I retook the test a few months later and passed with flying colours.

After a short time I had saved enough money to buy a bigger bike and was now the proud owner of a 650cc Matchless twin motorbike with a sports sidecar. I enjoyed riding thousands of miles all over the country, including going to Scotland for the New Year's Eve celebrations. My friends loved going in the sidecar, until an incident that left my passenger in fear of his life. We were enjoying a day out and had just joined the M1 motorway near Dunstable, when all of a sudden, I heard a loud 'CRACK' and to my horror the motorcycle and sidecar separated. I slowed and came to a stop on the hard shoulder of the motorway but the sidecar careered up the grass verge with the passenger displaying a look of horror on his face.

Fortunately, he safely came to a stop about 50 yards in front of me. I don't think he ever went in a sidecar again! I carried on riding the bike for the next few years but decided it might be safer without the sidecar.

After my biking days came to an end, I decided it would be the right time to take my car driving test. My brother Tommy was now working abroad as a telecommunications engineer and while he was away, he would let me look after his car. So after a few lessons I felt confident enough to book my test. As I arrived at the test centre, I couldn't believe my eyes when the examiner called my name – it was the same one who had taken me for my motorcycle test a few years previously. I must have made an impression on him as he said, 'Morning, Mr Sheridan. Can you read that number plate over there, and I hope you are not going to run over anyone today.' Luckily enough the test went without any hiccups and I passed first time.

I left Blundell's to work for Claridge and Hall, continuing to work on furniture but also house décor. I enjoyed my time working in this industry but unfortunately the money wasn't great so I decided to move on and in those days there were plenty of jobs, so I managed to get a position on the production line rubbing down and priming cars. Even though I was able to earn more money, I was still unsure what I wanted to do as a profession.

After two years I left Vauxhall Motors to join a government training scheme and trained as a plant fitter in Letchworth. I completed the training in six months, and with my new-found skills I was back off to Vauxhall but in a better position as I was employed as a pre-delivery check operative. This role meant I was tasked with repairing any faults in new cars that had just rolled off the production line. I enjoyed this job as it meant

I could take the new cars for a test drive after they had been repaired.

During this time, I met Betty. We started seeing each other after meeting at a friend's wedding. We immediately hit it off and it wasn't long before I proposed. Our wedding on 18 May 1968 was at St Thomas Church in Stopsley, with Tommy as my best man. We then moved into our first house in Cobden Street, Luton. It was a three-bedroomed terrace house with no bathroom, and despite the outside toilet we had so many happy memories there. It wasn't long before we were lucky enough to have our first child, my daughter Debbie. Another happy addition to the Sheridan family came two years later as my first son Andrew was born in 1970.

A couple of years after going back to Vauxhall, there was an opportunity within the company to gain an adult apprenticeship as a tool maker. This was a highly skilled job and there was plenty of competition. I managed to impress at the interview and was offered the role, for which part of the apprenticeship included going to college one day a week to learn subjects such as maths and technical drawing. This was a real bonus for me as it helped make up for the amount of time I had missed at school earlier in my life.

Even though my career at Vauxhall was going well I still missed the buzz and excitement of competitive sport. Before the accidents I was extremely active, would run everywhere and loved playing football. Since the accidents my sporting activities were almost zero, but this changed during my time at Vauxhall when myself and a colleague called Tony Beaumont decided to form a ten-pin bowling team. After recruiting one more employee, Bill Gentle, we started practising at the Greenways Bowl in Stopsley, Luton. Our team name was the Crestas after the famous Vauxhall car that was built at the plant. This was the time when ten-pin bowling was all the rage, so after hours and hours of practice there was a steady improvement and we discovered the team could play to a good standard. The Crestas became one of the most successful teams in Bedfordshire and won numerous trophies; finally, I could compete in competitive sport on an equal footing.

One night that sticks in my mind is a league decider. We had gone into the game in second place while our opponents were top, so whichever team won would be crowned champions. I had been going through a tough time as my father Thomas had been ill for a few months with terminal lung cancer. Two days before the final match he had taken a turn for the worse and I sat by his bedside as he tragically passed away at such a young age. Our family were devastated as we tried to come to terms with our loss, so I took some time off work to help Mum sort things out and support my brothers and beloved sisters Anne and Pat. My mind was in a daze and I had forgotten about everything else; my only focus was the family. On the day of the match I was sitting at home on the sofa when Mum said to me, 'John, what about your match tonight?' I replied, 'Mum, I don't want to play and leave you.' She told me, 'You need to go and play, it will do you good to leave the house for a couple of hours.' I decided to go but that night is still a blur and all I know is that my two mates must have played out of their skin as I was still in a daze and didn't contribute much. Somehow we won by a few pins and I'm sure Dad was looking over me that evening.

Unfortunately my two team-mates from that night have passed away. Tony became a lifelong friend; I had the honour of being his godfather even though he was older than me! He arranged to get married before he had been baptised so a last-minute baptism was organised, allowing the ceremony to take place. Over the years I have had the odd game of ten-pin bowling with my grandchildren and now and again I would get a strike, so my mind would sometimes drift and think of my two friends who carried me over the line that night to victory and helped me enjoy a couple of hours of normality at such a difficult time of my life.

By 1974 I was still at Vauxhall as a tool maker after completing the adult apprenticeship the previous year. The job involved making the die that produced the parts for the new vehicles. We had to work to extremely small tolerances and the die could take months to build. Even though I enjoyed engineering I still didn't feel that I had discovered my true vocation in life.

A good friend of mine told me that the local brewery, Whitbread, were looking for a cold store operative. This was a semi-skilled position that involved filtering, chilling and adding additives to the wide range of beers that the brewery produced. Part of the role also meant that you had to taste the beer to make sure it was okay! Despite this added bonus, the main thing that drew me to the position was the extra responsibility of working in the company surgery. I had experience of doing so while at Vauxhall and it was something I thoroughly enjoyed. The brewery was also a lot closer to my home, which meant I could cut down on the commute to work.

After attending an interview at the brewery I was told that subject to a medical the position was mine. I immediately accepted and after passing the medical I left my job at Vauxhall to start a new career at Whitbread. As soon as I walked through the door on that first day, I knew I had made the right decision. Whitbread were an excellent company to work for; they looked after their employees and provided a fantastic working environment. Each department had its own bar that could be used while at work, and we were even allowed two free pints per shift. During the next four years I can honestly say I loved every minute of my time there. As well as being a cold store operative I also became the company safety officer and industrial first aider. To enable me to undertake these responsibilities I had to attend numerous courses and when required I covered in the company surgery to treat any injuries or accidents.

And in 1974 my second son Paul was born, to join my other children Debbie and Andy. We also moved the same year to a new house; we loved our time at Cobden Street but it had become infested with mice due to the demolition of factories close by. With the arrival of Paul, we had also outgrown our home so it was time to move on. The council relocated us to a lovely new house at 12 Butely Road, and we bought the house a few years later while Margaret Thatcher was in power.

I would have been content to stay with Whitbread. In 1978 I was asked to take a supervisor's exam and attend an interview for a position at their plant in Magor, Wales. I was offered the position but it meant relocating, so I was given time to think it over with Betty. However, I was unaware that shortly my career was about to go in a different direction.

2

From Production Line to Professional Football

DURING MY time on the production line at Vauxhall Motors I met a lovely man called Pete Wyder. We shared a love of football and decided to start our own Sunday League club, Taverners. Pete was the manager and as I could no longer play, I took on the dual role of secretary and trainer. Pete, who sadly passed away recently, was an inspirational figure in local football and played a big part of my progress in those early years. This was my first step on a long road to a career in professional football, although at the time I had no idea where this road would take me.

That first season the team was made up mainly of Irish lads who liked a few drinks, and some Vauxhall reserve players. Pete was a workaholic; he would always be after better players and it wasn't long before we had attracted the cream of local talent. We had a great time building Taverners into one of the best teams in the county and had several successful years, including winning the Whitbread Cup eight times in 12 years from 1966.

Not long after starting Taverners I also joined the St John Ambulance division of Vauxhall Motors and trained to become an industrial first aider. I studied and worked hard, quickly developing a great love for first aid, and began to represent both Vauxhall and Bedfordshire in national competitions. We competed in both team and individual events against other St John divisions. We had an exceptional and knowledgeable team which consisted of Rex Hayward, Ken Rees, Eddie Edwards and myself. Due to our hard work and passion for first aid the team enjoyed a lot of success, culminating in lifting the prestigious winner of winners award in Cambridge. I also achieved individual success by being named the best St John Ambulance first aider in Bedfordshire.

I always felt very proud when putting on my St John brigade uniform, whether it was to compete in a first aid competition or to provide first aid support at a local event. Not long after joining I was extremely flattered to be asked by my divisional officer if I would be interested in training to become a lay instructor. This would allow me to teach first aid to various organisations and schools under the banner of this brilliant organisation. The first part of the process was to attend classes to learn first aid at the highest level and also how to master the intricacies of teaching. After an intense period of study, I managed to pass the first examination and moved on to the second part of the process, comprising of demonstrating your first aid skills, a Q&A and finally an assessment and lecture at the Luton headquarters in front of the county surgeon and the St John hierarchy.

The 30-minute lecture could be on your choice of subject but had to relate to anatomy, physiology or first aid and treatment. I opted for the skeletal system and after spending many hours researching and designing charts and meticulously making notes for the lecture, I was finally ready for my day of destiny – 27 August 1977. As I entered the lion's den that evening, I was met by the scrupulous eyes of the assessment panel and the many other Vauxhall divisions of the organisation. I was desperate to get off to a good start and find my rhythm, but as I introduced myself I was drowned out by a low-flying aeroplane from Luton airport. The short wait for the plane to pass over seemed to go on for ever and my anxiety grew with every passing second, and the situation didn't improve as when I tried to display my charts they kept falling to the floor. I must have looked like Frank Spencer trying to teach first aid.

However, I somehow managed to regain some composure and decided to forget about the charts and instead just use my notes for the presentation. As I opened my briefcase to take them out, my heart sank as I realised I had left them at home on the dining room table after a spot of last-minute revision. As they say, I was up the creek without a paddle and my confidence didn't improve as I looked at my divisional officer in the audience who was staring at the floor and shaking his head, and my team-mates were squirming in their seats feeling embarrassed for me.

Somehow I had to find a way out of this mess. Just to the right of me was a skeleton, so I had the brainwave of talking about sports injuries relating to the skeletal system. Everything I had prepared was now out of the window and the skeleton was my only hope. From the prospect of abject failure, a glimmer of hope raised my spirits as I dragged the dust-covered bones to the front of the hall but out of the corner of my eye I noticed the divisional officer mouth, 'What the f**k is this clown up to now?'

I loved being part of the St John Ambulance organisation and I wasn't going to go down without a fight. Starting from the skull, I tentatively began my lecture and after ten minutes I had grown into the situation. Despite the comedy routine at the beginning I was pleased to see the crowd had stayed with me and they looked mildly interested. I was also finding the lecture interesting as from each passing moment I had no idea what was going to come out of my mouth. Once I got into the flow of the topic, I was lost in the wonderful world of human anatomy. The time seemed to fly by and once I had got to the ankles I was well over my allotted period, so I decided to bring the lecture to a close. To my astonishment the county surgeon said, 'Please carry on. You have given us one of the most unusual lectures and have filled it with great information and you brought that skeleton to life. I could listen to you all evening.' I was delighted and was pleased to see my officer now nodding his head in approval instead of shaking it in despair. A round of applause followed and somehow I managed to get myself out of the crap.

A few weeks later I was overjoyed to be presented with the lay instructor certificate and over the following years I loved passing on my knowledge on the many courses I attended or at medical workshops at hospitals for doctors. I continued to lecture into my late 60s but without doubt that first talk still burns brightly in my mind.

Some people within Vauxhall and local football were getting to know that I had a love for first aid and the game. A Taverners player called Gerry Mullen also managed Vauxhall Motors' reserve team. One day after work, Gerry came to see me and asked if I would be interested in becoming the trainer for his team. The thought of moving into Saturday football hadn't really crossed my mind, but after much persuasion I agreed to give it a go. One of the main reasons for agreeing was that I really liked Gerry, a no-nonsense man who would always tell you the truth whether you liked it or not.

I enjoyed my first experience of senior football and felt comfortable with the lads. However, after only one match with the reserves I was asked by the first team manager to go with them for the next couple of games as their trainer had unfortunately fallen ill. I wasn't very keen in making the step up, as the first team included the majority of the best local players. Although Gerry wanted me to stay with the reserves, he thought it would be a good opportunity, so for the second time in as many weeks he persuaded me to give it a go. At that time Vauxhall Motors first team were a member of the Spartan League, which was a good standard of non-league football, and they also had their own ground and a playing surface that was the envy of many.

As I boarded the coach for that first game, I was filled with trepidation and wondered what I had let myself in for. It was a long journey from Luton to Surrey to play against Farnham Town. My fears were unfounded as from the first minute the lads made me feel extremely welcome, and luckily we ended up winning convincingly. It was a happy coach on the way back and we enjoyed a couple of drinks as we stopped at a restaurant for a meal. This really helped to break the ice and for me to get to know the players and management on a more personal level. I thoroughly enjoyed the day. I continued to go with the first team for a few more weeks as their normal trainer was still recovering from illness, and the players were getting used to me and accepted me for who I was. A short while later the committee asked if I would be prepared to stay with the first team for the remainder of the season. I agreed and actually ended up remaining in this role for the next four years.

During the early 1970s Vauxhall Motors were the biggest employer in Luton, taking on over 35,000 workers. The medical facilities in the factory were second to none and fortunately all of these were made available to the football club, so I had doctors, nurses, physiotherapists and an x-ray unit all at my disposal. The company fully subsidised both teams, so as well as the brilliant medical help and support in the factory I was also able to set up a small treatment room at the football ground. They paid for brand new medical equipment and a plunge bath for hydrotherapy. I was in my element, treating players, planning remedial programmes and also introducing warm-ups on the pitch before a match. These were a new experience for the players, and I'm sure a few of the other local physios thought I was mad with the new innovations and ideas I introduced.

During this time the team enjoyed a very successful spell. We consistently finished high in the league, won a couple of prestigious cup finals and enjoyed a long run in the FA Cup. Along the way we managed to beat teams from much higher leagues but finally succumbed to Bishop's Stortford who went on to reach the second round proper before losing to Peterborough United. And it wasn't just the club that was getting recognition as I remember after a home game we were having a drink in the famous Vauxhall green hut (this hut was equivalent to the famous Anfield boot room as it was by invitation only!) Our club secretary came in and said, 'Well done, John, you have been selected as physio for the Spartan League representative side.' This was a great honour and made me realise how far I had come in such a short time. Two of our players had also been selected for the rep game against London University. I felt immensely proud, not just for myself but also the other two lads as we flew the flag for Vauxhall Motors.

My time with the first team wasn't always a bed of roses and I remember an incident that could only happen in non-league football. One evening I was competing in the Bedfordshire first aid competition, but it unfortunately clashed with our Bedfordshire Senior Cup semi-final against one of our local rivals. Luckily the first aid competition was being held not too far from the game, so I worked out I could miss the first half, finish the competition then rush as quickly as I could to the match.

I arrived just after half-time and as I walked across the car park still wearing my St John Ambulance uniform, my attention was drawn to a confrontation between two people. One was a well-dressed, distinguished-looking man and to my horror the other was the Vauxhall manager. As I approached the pair there was a tussle and the well-dressed man fell to the floor clutching his leg. I rushed over to make sure he was okay, and as I started to examine his leg it felt extremely hard. It took me a moment to realise that it was actually an artificial leg! I helped him to his feet while trying to calm him down and defuse the situation. He told me the reason he fell was because he was kicked. I thought the bad tackles were meant for the pitch but seemingly our manager was showing the team how it should be done!

In all seriousness I couldn't believe he would do such a thing; someone reported the incident and after an investigation a disciplinary hearing was arranged by the county FA. I had been called as a witness so travelled to the hearing with the team manager, but unfortunately my testimony didn't help and he was found guilty of improper conduct. As a punishment he received a lengthy ban. The man with the false leg turned out to be the local mayor and as we left, he thanked me for giving evidence and for being one of the only witnesses to tell the truth. As you can imagine, the car journey home to Luton was a quiet one. Undeterred, the manager found a way of attending home games as he would poke his head over the hedge to give instructions. Luckily for me and the hedges his ban was lifted a few weeks later and he proudly took his place back in the dugout.

My time spent in the Spartan League with Vauxhall was extremely enjoyable and it certainly helped me on my way to a career in the Football League. However, the more experience I gained the more I wanted to test myself at a higher level. An opportunity to do so came along one day while at work in the factory. I had just qualified as a tool maker and was at my bench in the die shop when I heard a voice say, 'Hello John, do you fancy a challenge?' I looked up and it was one of Bedfordshire's most successful non-league managers, Gordon Todd. Toddy had been on Liverpool's books as a youngster and despite being released, he enjoyed a good playing career before hanging his boots up for management. He said, 'Tring Town want me to go and sort them out. They are languishing near the bottom of the league and I am going to be their new manager. I want you to come with me as physio and my old mate Gordon Brown is joining to do the coaching.' It was a difficult decision but the lure of stepping up a level into the Isthmian League was too big to turn down, so with a heavy heart I decided to leave Vauxhall Motors FC.

When I first walked into the ground at Tring, in the heart of the beautiful Hertfordshire countryside, I was relieved to find a friendly club that was well organised and had a hard-working committee. The club enjoyed close links to Watford FC as a couple of board members were associated with both teams. Unfortunately, some of the players weren't as friendly before my first game. As the lads got changed I told them we would be going out for a warm-up on the pitch, which was alien to some and they abruptly told me they weren't going to join in. I knew the importance and benefits of a thorough warm-up so said, 'That's fine, but those of you that don't join in, take your kit off and go home as you aren't playing.' The dressing room was in uproar and plenty of hostile words were aimed in my direction. All of a sudden Toddy burst in and said, 'What is the problem, John?' I replied, 'I haven't got a problem. Some of the lads won't join in with the warm-up so I've told them they aren't playing.'

Toddy was brilliant. He backed me 100 per cent and said, 'If they apologise to you, John, can they play?' I replied, 'Of course, as long as they do the warm-up.' That did the trick and I received some half-hearted apologies, but most importantly all of the players joined me on the pitch and had a really good warm-up. The game started and the players were on fire, performing with much more intensity and power which resulted in us scoring early before going on to win convincingly. After the game, a couple of the lads came to see me and said, 'Sorry John, the warm-up was great and from now on you won't get any problems from us.' They were true to their word and I was quickly accepted by the lads. We enjoyed a great working relationship and they were a fantastic group to deal with. Within that squad was a certain player called Bradley Walsh, who went on to enjoy fame as an actor, comedian and TV presenter. Looking back there were a few other comedians in that team as well!

An incident that will always stay with me happened one evening after training at Tring. I left the club for my trip home to Luton through the dark country lanes of Hertfordshire. Five minutes into my journey I drove around a sharp left-hand bend and to my horror was confronted with a car that had just crashed head-first into a tree. I immediately stopped sharply and rushed across and as I got closer, I realised there was somebody sitting motionless in the driver's seat. I quickly opened the door and examined him; he was still alive but unconscious and in a bad way.

If matters couldn't get any worse, I looked up and noticed smoke bellowing from the bonnet. The enormity of the situation hit me and I was petrified, but the adrenaline kicked in and I was faced with a big decision. Should I stay with him and potentially both of us could go up in flames or should I take the risk of moving him to safety? There was only one choice I could make, so with immense caution I moved him as quickly and as safely as possible to a safe distance away from the car. As I was doing this, somebody else had stopped to see if I needed any assistance. I asked him to find a phone box and call for help. Within no time at all an ambulance and fire engine arrived to take over from me. As the fireman made the car safe and the driver was taken to hospital, I slipped away unnoticed but still shaking with fear. I later found out he thankfully made a full recovery, but for a long time afterwards I suffered nightmares imagining what could have happened to us both if the car had exploded.

After a couple of seasons Gordon Todd left to take over as manager at his old club Shefford FC. He asked me to go with him but I was enjoying myself at Tring so decided to stay on. The appointment of the new Tring manager was shrouded in mystery as the committee told myself and the players to report to training as normal on Tuesday and we would finally discover who was taking over. I arrived at the club early to get the lads ready for training, and after they had gone out to train I started to treat a player who was recovering from a long-term injury. He had undergone a meniscectomy to his knee – the removal of a portion of one of the cartilages due to a tear or other damage. Suddenly the door of the treatment room burst open and a giant of a man stood in the doorway. With no introduction he abruptly said, 'What is wrong with him?' I told him and he then said, 'He looks okay to me. Get him out training.' I was fuming, so said, 'I don't know who you are but get out of my treatment room. Next time you want to come in then make sure you knock.' With that he turned around and walked out.

The player I was treating turned and looked me, then said, 'John, I think that was the new manager.' I thought to myself that my time at Tring was over with but at least my integrity was intact. Suddenly there was a knock on the door and in walked the same man, who said, 'Hi, I am John Delaney, the new manager. When do you think he will be ready to return to training?' I replied, 'Nice to meet you. I am John Sheridan, the physio. As soon as he is ready to train again, you will be the first to know.' John then shook my hand and I said, 'Thanks, John, I am sure we will get on really well. Can I buy you a drink after training so we can have a chat and get to know each other?' We developed a good working relationship and our initial meeting was never mentioned. I believe you have to set your stall out at the beginning and I was more than prepared to put my coat on and slip away into the night.

Before we met, I didn't know too much about John but I later discovered he had enjoyed a fantastic career and won 17 England non-league caps. He had been the captain at Wycombe Wanderers and also had a couple of years at Bournemouth as a professional. I enjoyed working with him and found him a very likeable man and still a fine player.

Over the past few years I had worked hard with St John Ambulance, gaining an extensive knowledge of first aid, but due to my increased involvement in football I realised I wanted and needed to improve my knowledge of sports injuries. I discovered that the FA ran a treatment of injury course which was predominantly aimed at trainers/physios from the professional game. It was held at Lilleshall over three years, including a two-week residential period. Unfortunately it cost a lot of money, which I couldn't really afford especially as I had a young family. However, Betty understood how much this course meant to me and pushed me to try, so with the help of my players at Vauxhall Motors and Taverners, who unbeknown to me kindly had a collection, I had enough money to enrol and just enough left over to buy the relevant medical books.

I arrived at Lilleshall on the first day with great trepidation, alongside my good friend Craig Simmons, who was starting his second year. A few years later, Craig went on to become a highly regarded member of the FA medical department throughout his numerous years of service. The vast majority of the 35 candidates were full-time staff from professional clubs such as Chelsea, Manchester City, Arsenal and Leeds, as well as teams from the lower reaches of the Football League. Generally, almost all of the lads on the course would support each other and I went on to follow their careers with interest over the years that followed. However, I did get a few negative comments in those early days at Lilleshall. I remember one occasion one of my fellow candidates said to me in his broad Yorkshire accent, 'John, what is someone like you doing on this course? You have no chance of working in the Football League.' To this day I am not completely sure what he really meant. Was it because of my limp or was it because I was a non-league physio? At the time the comment hurt me but I thought of my family and all the people who had helped me get on the course. His words made me more determined to prove all the doubters wrong and gain that prestigious qualification.

The syllabus for the course was devised by the FA and delivered in the main by the brilliant Paddy Armour and his very able assistants. Alongside tutoring for the FA, Paddy was the head of the physiotherapy department at Pinderfields Hospital in Wakefield and also physio for the Great Britain and Wakefield rugby league teams. My room-mate for the two-week residential was Alan Smith, who went on to become the physio for Sheffield Wednesday and later England. We instantly struck up a great friendship and shared the same desire to succeed and philosophy of working extremely hard, so we would often study all day and long into the night. Despite the initial negative comments, I started to gain respect from the other candidates and even played in goal in one of the small-sided games with some of the old pros.

One of the main memories I have of my time at Lilleshall happened after a hard day studying. As I was leaving the classroom with Alan, my tutor Geoff Ladley stopped me and said, 'John, in the morning I want you to present to the class all the muscles of the lower leg, their origins and insertions, nerves and major blood supply.' I couldn't believe it. Why me, I thought. It was a difficult task but instead of feeling sorry for myself I decided to revise through the night to make sure I was up to the challenge. By the time morning came around I was confident I knew all of the information, but to present it to the class I would have to talk uninterrupted so not to lose the flow. I entered the classroom and with 34 pairs of eyes staring at me immediately started the presentation.

Halfway through, Geoff stopped me and said, 'John, that is not correct, you have given some wrong information.' I wanted to keep the thread of the talk going, so replied, 'Can you let me continue and tell me where I went wrong when I am finished?' When the presentation came to an end, Geoff told myself and my classmates the mistake before allowing us to go for a tea break. Just before we left the classroom, he asked the other candidates for a show of hands to see if I was right or wrong. Thirty-three hands went up to say I had got it wrong and only one hand went up to agree that I was right – my room-mate Alan. Geoff then said to us both, 'You had better get ready to apologise when you come back in.' After the break, we had all returned to the class when Geoff said to me, 'I will give you a chance to admit you were wrong.' Throughout the break I had gone over the presentation in my mind and was sure I hadn't made a mistake, so replied, 'No, Geoff, I'm sorry but I am right and you are wrong.' I thought I was going to get an almighty bollocking for disagreeing as he started to frown and shake his head, then suddenly he started to smile, walked over and shook my hand and said, 'Well done John, you are right. I will make a physio out of you.' The class looked on in astonishment – this lovely guy had been deliberately hard on me to see what I was made of.

I was desperate to pass the course so over the next two years I continued to study extremely hard and gained some valuable extra experience while volunteering at the Luton & Dunstable Hospital. This held me in good stead and although the dropout rate of the course was extremely high, I loved every minute of it. The final part of the course consisted of two written examinations, a practical examination and an interview with the tutors where they would question you on your thesis. There was no doubt that if you were going to gain your qualification you had to earn it. On 8 July 1974, all the hard work paid off when I was delighted to receive a certificate through the post informing me that I had passed the course. I was relieved but so pleased and proud of myself.

The hard work over the past few years was starting pay off and I had been selected as physio for England Schoolboys, and the representative teams of the Bedfordshire FA, Spartan League and North Home Counties Sunday League. I also joined the Society of Remedial Gymnasts. In 1978 I was lucky enough to win the highly coveted North Home Counties Sportsman Award for services to Taverners and the league. Somehow I also found time to lecture first aid for the FA and act as physio for the ex-professional players who were undertaking the residential coaching courses at Lilleshall.

It was a great honour to be involved with the England Schoolboys team. I acted as physio for both the regional trials and for the final squad at a week-long training camp. This camp culminated in a home international match against either Scotland, Ireland or Wales, but I missed out on the trips to Wembley because to attend the games you had to be a school teacher. The man in charge of the squad at this time was the very likeable Dave 'Harry' Bassett, who later became famous for his exploits with the 'Crazy Gang' at Wimbledon.

There is one story that sticks in my mind from a training camp, held at the Grade II-listed estate at Newland Park in Chalfont St Peter. This camp is etched in my mind as it was in August 1977, and while we were there came the news that shocked the world with the announcement of Elvis Presley's death. After a long day on the training pitch, we met up for evening dinner and having finished eating, I told Dave and his coaches that I had a few injuries to treat and afterwards I would settle down in my room for the night. However, Dave told me they were planning to go over to the common room for a drink and invited me to join them. This was my first visit to Newland Park, a large estate, and I had no idea where the common room was located. Dave gave me directions, so after finishing the treatment I decided to wander over for a quick drink.

After a short walk I came across what I assumed was the common room so I walked up to the door, found it unlocked and went straight in. There was no sign of Dave or his staff so I decided to make myself comfy and wait for them to turn up. After five minutes I started to feel thirsty so decided to make myself a cup of tea, then found some biscuits and settled down on the sofa to watch TV and wait for the others. After about an hour there was still no sign of them so I came to the conclusion that they must have changed their minds. As I was leaving, I was still a bit peckish so decided to take a couple of pieces of fruit from the fruit bowl to enjoy when I returned to my room.

After a good night's sleep, I went down for breakfast the next morning and sat down with Dave and his staff. He said, 'Where did you get to last night?' I replied, 'I went to the house to meet you but nobody turned up. I waited for a while then went back to my room.' Dave started laughing and said, 'You muppet, you went to the wrong place. I have just been told by the estate security that the owners of the house have reported that they have been burgled by a very hungry burglar!' He didn't let me forget it for a very long time!

Even though I was heavily involved in football and busy lecturing on first aid for the FA, I had no desire to work in the professional game. In 1979 myself and Betty were still agonising over moving to Wales when after returning from a night shift at Whitbread the phone rang for a call that was going to change my life.

3

In at the Deep End

ON THE other end of the phone was David Pleat, the young Luton town manager. Their physio had recently left the club and he was looking for a replacement. I had been recommended to him by someone who knew me from my role as safety officer at Whitbread. David asked me to come down to Kenilworth Road for an interview with himself and assistant manager Ken Gutteridge. The thought of entering the harsh world of professional football made me feel extremely anxious. I didn't know how I would react to running on to the field with a pronounced limp in front of thousands of people. This gave me a dilemma but after much soul-searching, I realised I had nothing to lose and agreed to go for the interview.

Without much expectation I went to meet David and Ken. Ken was well respected within the game and throughout his coaching career had worked with some of the best managers in the business. I was nervous as I walked through the door of the manager's office, but they both quickly put me at ease. The interview was going well and we talked about my career in non-league football and medical qualifications, but I took offence to one of Ken's questions. He said, 'Do you know how to treat a broken leg?' I replied, 'I am wasting my time here. If you need to ask me that then you don't know much about me.' David reassured me they had done their research and it was just a routine question. As the interview was coming to an end, I decided to be completely honest with David and Ken regarding my anxiety and concerns about being the first physio in the Football League to run on to the pitch with a limp. Even though David said it wasn't an issue for him, I was still unsure if I wanted the job so replied, 'I'm sure you will find a more suitable candidate than me, but if you are really struggling, I can help out with the reserves.' I felt relieved as I left Kenilworth Road and did not for one minute expect to hear back from them.

As I drove home, I thought about what had happened over the past couple of hours. I was pleased that I went to meet David and Ken but was more than happy to go back to local football and also explore the possibility of moving to Wales to take up the supervisor's role with Whitbread. When I got home, Betty asked how it had gone. I replied, 'It was okay but I'm not expecting to get the job.' A few hours later the phone rang and the voice explained, 'Hi John, it's David Pleat, I would like to offer you the position of physio with Luton Town. I was impressed with your honesty and understand your anxiety but I am convinced you are the right man for the job.' I was shocked. My fears hadn't subsided so I asked David for a bit of time to consider the offer. After much thought and discussion with Betty, who has always been my rock and the sensible one, we decided that if I didn't give it a go then I would regret it for the rest of my life. So I phoned David and accepted the job. He then told me that the role also consisted of being the kit man and looking after the players' welfare. As I had already booked a family holiday to Majorca, it was agreed that I would start immediately upon my return.

My first day at Luton Town arrived in July 1979 and I awoke with much trepidation about how the day would pan out. I had never met any of the players before and wondered how they would react to having a physio with a limp. My worries were unfounded as from day one everyone at the club was extremely welcoming and friendly. The morning flew by and I immediately felt at home looking after the injured players. As lunchtime approached, I had just finished treating Ricky Hill when he asked if I would like something to eat. Due to skipping breakfast that morning after feeling anxious, I realised I was absolutely starving, so myself and Ricky set off to the local fish and chip shop. On the way we had a great chat and got to know each other; this gesture certainly helped ease any nerves that were still lingering. Ricky was and always has been a gentleman. He is a club legend and a fantastic footballer who, in my opinion, should have been capped more times for England.

Despite the initial intrigue about my limp the players quickly accepted me for who I was. As the season went on they soon realised that I was someone who cared passionately about them and their welfare. In those early years the players were very kind to me and I quickly developed a close bond with them, especially the great characters such as Ricky, Brian Stein, David Moss, Kirk Stephens, Mal Donaghy and Jake Findlay to name just a few. I found that talking and listening to them about any problems inside or outside of football only deepened our working relationship and they quickly became friends and trusted me completely. I knew David Pleat was keen for me not to get too close to the players but I felt it could only benefit him and the club to create a happy and trusting environment. I don't believe in tittle-tattle from either the players or staff while in the treatment room; confidentiality and trust was the key. This stood me in good stead throughout my career in football over the next 30-plus years.

The staff were also fantastic towards me and I soon became hardened to the day-to-day workings at a professional football club. I enjoyed the great sense of humour and banter that came with it. We had a real tight-knit group of players and staff. David was a superb astute manager alongside coaches David Coates, Ken Gutteridge and John Moore, all of whom have forgotten more about football than most people will ever know, and of course the inspirational ex-West Ham player Trevor Hartley who was a fantastic coach and is still a great friend up to the present day. Another man I built up a great relationship with was our club doctor Bill Berry, a fellow new recruit that summer. Our relationship flourished from day one. Bill is a lovely man and has a great depth of knowledge and from 1979 until I left in 1986 we enjoyed a close, trusting and respectful friendship.

Even though I settled in quickly, I still felt extremely anxious about running on to the pitch. I remember our first league game of the season at home against Oldham Athletic. As I walked out of the tunnel towards the dugouts I was shaking with fear and as white as a ghost! I kept asking myself, 'What will the supporters think when they see me run on to the pitch and realise they have the only limping physio in the Football League?' To my relief I didn't have to go on in that first match, and amazingly the wait continued as I didn't have to run on for the first five games!

However, on 16 September, our sixth game of the season, I finally had to tread the hallowed turf of Kenilworth Road. One of our players went down injured and as I went on to treat him, the home fans gave me a great reception. I was pleased to finally get it over and done with. Due to the continued support of the Luton fans my confidence slowly grew, but I soon started to get noticed by opposition followers. I received different levels of abuse depending on who our opponents were or what ground we were playing at. At first it hurt but after a while I realised that to have a successful career in professional football I had to toughen up and embrace the crowd. So whenever I would receive some stick from the fans, I would respond to them by waving or pretending to doff my cap. This seemed to work and helped me build up a good rapport with supporters at numerous away grounds.

Although it didn't take me long to get use to the banter from the terraces, I wasn't prepared for receiving stick from an unlikely source. I remember one particular bruising encounter that season, when I lost count of the amount of times I had to go on to the pitch. The next morning, I went to Kenilworth Road to treat the injured players and on the way I stopped at the local newsagent to buy the Sunday papers for the lads to read. Before they arrived, I grabbed a cup of tea and sat down to have a quick read. As I turned the back page to look for the report of our game the previous afternoon, I was amazed to see the headline 'Luton had so many injuries even their physio was limping!' It was a cheap laugh at my expense, and at the time I didn't take a lot of notice but I imagine that deep down I was hurt. Unbeknown to me, a lot of people had taken offence to the article and flooded the newspaper with complaints, then a few days later I received a letter from the sports reporter apologising for it.

I also experienced racial discrimination for the first time that season. We were playing away when with 15 minutes to go David Pleat asked me to make a substitution. I held up the player's number and as he came off the pitch, I gave him a tracksuit top to keep warm. We returned to the dugout and both sat down to watch the remainder of the game. Suddenly a supporter popped his head round the side of the dugout and shouted at the player, 'You black bastard.' I was livid so quickly jumped up and grabbed him by the throat and said, 'Don't you dare call him that. I will see you after the game to sort it out.' He looked shocked and sat back down.

The final whistle blew and I walked back towards the tunnel with the rest of the staff but lo and behold that same supporter was waiting for me with his mates. As I got ready for a confrontation, I was marched up the tunnel and told in no uncertain terms by Ken Gutteridge to get in the dressing room and to never get involved with spectators. After making sure the players were okay and any injuries were patched up, Ken asked to speak to me. He then proceeded to give me an almighty telling-off and told me that this was my one and only chance. The player I was trying to protect came to thank me but told me not to do it again.

I also remember at some away grounds bananas being thrown at players, but naively I didn't expect this level of abuse in professional football. What a sad indictment of the game. I began to realise that some ignorant people think they can pay to watch live football and feel it gives them the right to shout vulgar and racist remarks at the players. Unfortunately, this still seems part of our game today.

The players quickly realised I cared for them but it didn't stop them trying to play an initiation trick on me. Our first overnight trip of the season was against Cardiff City on 6 October 1979. We set off on Friday lunchtime for the long journey to Wales and arrived at the hotel just outside Cardiff that evening. After unpacking my clothes, the next task was to set up a mini treatment room in my bedroom as some of the players had slight knocks. After dinner I went back upstairs to get ready for the lads but as I approached my hotel room, I noticed the door was slightly ajar. I wondered if somebody was in there so I pushed it open slowly to investigate and immediately saw a bucket of water perched on top of the door! I closed it carefully so the bucket stayed in the same position. A short while later one of the players pushed the door open expecting to see their new physio looking like a drowned rat, but unfortunately for him he got a shock as he felt the full force of the bucket and ice cold water. The lads never tried again!

Looking back on my first season in professional football, it was extremely enjoyable but definitely a steep learning curve. It was hard to juggle the responsibilities of the role, which included treating all of the professional and apprentice players, rehabilitation of injuries, looking after the players' welfare and – the worst job for me – being responsible for the kit room. I didn't enjoy the job of kit man, so to help I roped in some of the apprentices to pack the skips for matchdays, but unfortunately on more than one occasion we arrived at an away game with boots and kit missing as the young lads hadn't packed them properly.

I remember on one occasion, at West Ham, I went to Upton Park early to prepare for the game and hang up the kit. David had already named the side so the last job was to put the players' boots alongside the correct shirt. Unfortunately I discovered that one pair of boots had not been packed by the apprentices and the only spare pair were mine! When the players arrived at the ground, I had to break the bad news and explain the boots had been left behind at Kenilworth Road and the only option was for him to wear mine. After the game I asked him if the boots were okay. He said they made his feet a bit sore and had caused him to limp. I said, 'Are you taking the piss?!'

When you arrived back at the ground late on a Saturday night after an away game you would have to unpack the kit and boots to stop them smelling. I remember the early days at Luton, we would turn on the lights to take the skips back into the dressing room and be greeted by hundreds of cockroaches scuttling to get away to safety.

I felt the additional responsibility of kit man wasn't allowing me to give 100 per cent concentration to my passion and love of physiotherapy. I was becoming tired and not spending as much time as I would have liked with my family, so something had to change. At the end of the first season I spoke with David Pleat and told him of my concerns. David was brilliant and completely understood, so he agreed it would be beneficial for the club to appoint a full-time kit man. We were lucky to find George Rogers who took over the role. Nothing was too much trouble for George and he quickly became a valued member of staff. Throughout his life George carried out a variety of roles for the club. He was also well known in local football and was a great help to me over the years. A real unsung hero.

Despite David knowing that my full attention was directed towards the players' welfare and physiotherapy, he would still sometimes try to give me extra responsibility. One morning the phone rang in the treatment room and on the other end of the line was the manager, asking if everything was okay. 'Yes, boss,' I replied. He continued, 'John, all of the scouts are busy so I need you to go and watch a striker tonight at one of the Midlands non-league clubs.' I was a bit taken aback so asked, 'Why do you want me to go and watch him?' David responded abruptly, 'To go and see if he is any good!' Deep down he knew that I didn't want to get involved in the football side of the club, so I replied, 'David, I know nothing about football but I will go and watch him and report back to you if he gets injured, what time it occurs and the extent of the injury.' He said, 'You won't change, will you,' and promptly put the phone down. That was the end of my promising scouting career!

Another time David tried to get me involved in tactics and coaching was when the team came in at half-time losing 2-0 after a poor first-half performance. I was quietly going from player to player sorting out and patching up any medical problems. David was giving his team talk when he suddenly turned to me and said, 'You are quiet, John, what do you think of that abysmal display?' I stopped what I was doing, looked up and realised the dressing room had gone silent as the players waited for my words of wisdom. After a short pause I replied, 'David, I know f**k all about football, I am here to look after their injuries not coach them!' I noticed the players were trying not to laugh and the atmosphere in the dressing room seemed to lift. David then said, 'You know much more about football than you let on.' Maybe the change of mood at half-time gave them a boost as the lads went out in the second half, played much better and grabbed a late winner.

These two stories raise a controversial question. Should physiotherapists get involved in football? In my humble opinion the answer is a definite no. My belief is that a physio is there to look after the wellbeing and welfare of players, to treat their injuries and be a father figure that they can trust and confide in. I believe that people sometimes forget professional footballers are only human beings; they have the same concerns and anxieties as us and there are numerous distractions inside and outside of football that can cause a loss of form. If I had been bellowing from the touchline at them for playing badly or discussing a poor performance in the treatment room, then I would be the last person they would confide in.

During my time in football I have known physios who have been involved in coaching or scouting. Dave Butler, my assistant at Spurs, would often go and watch a player for Terry Venables, but as an ex-professional he was better equipped and had an interest in doing so. I have always loved football and been involved in thousands of games from grassroots to the Premier League. This has given me a great knowledge of the game I love but throughout my career I have always tried to keep football and physiotherapy separate. This philosophy has helped me build trusting relationships with players at all levels of the game and enabled me to assist them on both a personal and professional level.

4

Surgeons, Injuries
and Professor Smillie

THE EIGHT years I spent at Luton Town took me from being a naive young physio to an experienced club physiotherapist with a thirst for knowledge. I continued to study physiotherapy and sports medicine, and with the amalgamation of the Society of Remedial Gymnasts and Recreational Therapy with the Chartered Society of Physiotherapy in 1985 I qualified to become a highly respected chartered physiotherapist. Not too bad for someone who had missed out on a large part of his schooling, but it shows that if you have determination and a hunger to succeed you can achieve your dreams.

To help me gain a better understanding of injuries, I would always attend any operations on my players. This also allowed me to build up a trusted network of excellent specialists and I am forever grateful they allowed me into their operating theatres to watch them at work.

My knowledge of living anatomy was being enhanced in a way I could only have ever dreamed about. Watching these operations helped me plan the rehabilitation protocols for the player but just as important they knew I was there for them, making sure they were okay and contacting their families with any news.

Some of my experiences during this spell in my career were not always glamorous but were extremely memorable. Early on in my Luton career, our highly rated central defender Mick Saxby accidentally collided with a team-mate and sustained an awful knee injury. Myself and Dr Berry couldn't get to the bottom of the problem as Mick continually broke down during his rehabilitation. We took him to see several consultants and he had numerous arthroscopies (this was quite a new procedure at the time – minimal invasive surgery to allow an examination of a joint).

Mick was desperate to get fit and back playing but unfortunately we were getting nowhere fast. I had recently been reading a book on the knee by Professor Ian Smillie and although he was nearing the end of his career, he had gained a worldwide reputation in knee surgery and was one of the first super-specialists. I had a brainwave; even though he lived in Scotland I realised he was the person who could help me, so I asked the club secretary Wendy to try and find some contact details for this great man. A short while later the phone rang in the treatment room – it was Wendy, and somehow she had managed to get the phone number for Professor Smillie in a small hamlet of Dundee. The next morning I plucked up enough courage and called him at home, which was completely unethical but I was a desperate physio! He answered the phone and I started to explain the problem, so he said, 'Does your doctor know you have phoned me at home?' 'Of course,' I replied through gritted teeth.

My call worked. This kind man must have heard the desperation in my voice and agreed to give me an appointment in a couple of weeks. We had just won the Second Division championship and the appointment coincided with the celebration party, so instead of enjoying a few drinks with the rest of the staff and squad, myself and Mick found ourselves on an overnight sleeper train to Dundee to hopefully find an answer to our injury nightmare. The morning came and with not much sleep and bloodshot eyes we arrived in the Dundee rain. With time to kill and feeling hungry we managed to eat breakfast at a local bus garage. We picked up the hire car nearby and then travelled to the Fernbrae Nursing Home for our appointment with fate.

As soon as we entered Professor Smillie's consulting room he radiated an aura of confidence as he gave a methodical examination of Mick. I then told him the complete record of the injury, the treatment – both surgical and remedial – and confirmed there had been no steroid injections. He took me to one side and told me he knew the problem and would write to the club doctor and consultant with his findings. I was relieved that we had finally unearthed the issue but due to the seriousness of the injury I was desperate for this great surgeon to carry out the procedure. I asked him if he would be prepared to operate but he refused, saying, 'I no longer perform many operations.' If Mick stood any chance of playing football again then Professor Smillie was our only hope, so undeterred I pleaded for him to reconsider. He must have felt sorry for me as after a short pause he changed his mind and agreed to operate in a week's time.

Upon returning home the next day I decided to tell Dr Berry what had happened and the lengths I had been to. He said, 'You are out of order the way you went about it.' However, as he left the treatment room, he turned to me with a twinkle in his eye and with a broad smile said, 'Well done John, I don't know how you managed to get one of the greatest surgeons in the world to operate on our player.' A week later myself and

Mick made our way back up to Dundee for the operation. Our goalkeeper at the time at Luton was the talented Jake Findlay, whose parents lived close to Dundee in Blairgowrie, and they kindly let me stay with them for a couple of nights and made me feel most welcome.

As we prepared for the operation the theatre sister allowed me to watch Professor Smillie at work. He made his incision very carefully and then slowly raised the patella, which was where all the pain was coming from, and to my amazement a flap of articular cartilage dropped down. This had not been seen during the arthroscopy due to the pressure of the solution which extends the knee to allow the surgeon to look thoroughly, resulting in the offending piece of cartilage being positioned correctly during the procedure. When the solution was released at the end of the arthroscopy, the damaged piece of cartilage would drop down and cause the pain due to the bone being exposed.

After the surgery had finished, Professor Smillie paid me the greatest compliment when he said, 'John, sit down with me, we will have a cup of tea together and discuss the operation.' So, while still in our gowns, he picked up his famous book of the knee and kindly spent an hour explaining what he had done, what to expect during the rehabilitation and other injuries and issues that he had experienced during his long and distinguished career as an expert in this field. I was mesmerised and listened to his every word; he also answered the many questions I asked him. Upon returning to Luton, I told Dr Berry how Professor Smillie had given up his time to give me a small insight into his knowledge. Dr Berry said, 'Do you realise how lucky you were to spend time with the world's greatest expert on the knee?' I certainly realised that due to this kind gentleman giving up some of his invaluable time and experience I had returned from Scotland a better physiotherapist.

Mick and I continued to work hard on his rehabilitation. Even though we had the world's leading knee authority operate on him, the horrific nature of this injury was proving hard to overcome. During the writing of this book, I spoke to Mick to get his thoughts on this time in his life. This is what he told me, 'I just remember it being the lowest point, not only in my football career but also my life. Football was all I ever wanted to do. I remember it being the first serious injury I ever had and it ended up finishing my career. Although John remained positive, I was really struggling with my mental health and it did not help that the team were flying. You never felt part of things when you were out injured. I will always remain grateful to John for all his efforts and support during the worst time in my life. I will always be thinking "what if?"'

A lot of credit goes to Mick as somehow against all odds, he did manage to recover enough to play professionally again for clubs such as Grimsby Town and Middlesbrough, unfortunately only a handful of times. I am sure that this unusual but horrendous injury ultimately finished his career at an early age. Throughout all my time in football and in private practice, I didn't experience this injury ever again. I genuinely believe that even with all the medical advances that are available today, it would still most probably end a player's career.

Sometimes when you are trying to get a player fit from injury, help can come from the unlikeliest source. Shortly after joining Luton I discovered that one of our key players, David Moss, was suffering from a long-term issue with a persistent lower abdominal groin strain. Mossy had worked hard and strengthened the area during rehabilitation, but unfortunately kept breaking down in training and matches. Luckily a follow-up appointment had already been booked with his consultant. We made the difficult trip to central London and as we entered the consulting room, we both sat down. He turned to David and asked, 'How are you?' David replied, 'I am still in discomfort, can't play football and have difficulty sleeping.' To my amazement the consultant said, 'Well you had better carry on resting then.' We were then shown the door without even an examination. After travelling all that way to see him I was astonished that the appointment lasted less than two minutes and promised myself that I would never take a player to see him again.

We were still no nearer getting David fit, then inspiration came from the most unexpected of directions. One of the players had left a copy of *Shoot!* in the dressing room, so at the end of a long day I sat down and decided to flick through it. I read an article about a Birmingham City player who had seemingly suffered a similar injury, made a full recovery and was now back playing. As a long shot I decided to call the Birmingham physio to get some advice, and he kindly told me the surgeon who had operated on his player was called Mr Polyzoides. So the following day I called him and explained the issues we were having. He said, 'It sounds as if your player has developed a tear of the external oblique aponeurosis.' I had no idea what he was talking about as I had never heard of this injury before. Luckily, Mr Polyzoides agreed to operate on David the following week. Mossy made a full recovery and was straight back in the first team within eight weeks.

At the time little was known about this injury and shortly afterwards I discovered that numerous players had been treated in a variety of different ways, most of which had proved unsuccessful. One surgeon in particular, Jerry Gilmore, had also identified this issue of long-standing chronic groin pain. This injury later became known as 'Gilmore's Groin' due to the success of Mr Gilmore's diagnosis, surgery and rehabilitation. He was a great man and surgeon and we instantly gained a mutual respect. A few years later I was very privileged to become consultant physiotherapist in his practice in Harley Street, specialising in the rehabilitation of this injury.

The players of today are generally much fitter due to the increased knowledge and understanding of diets, training methods and fitness coaches. However, I don't believe the injuries modern footballers suffer are any different to those sustained during the five decades I enjoyed in the game. But with the advancement of diagnostic equipment, surgical techniques and the expertise of surgeons, therapists and medical staff have changed the way rehabilitation is undertaken. Due to this many players' careers have been saved when in the past their livelihoods would have finished prematurely.

A good example of this is the anterior cruciate ligament injury that Brian Clough sustained in a match on Boxing Day in 1962. Brian enjoyed a career as a striker with Middlesbrough and Sunderland, scoring 251 goals from 274 starts. In a match against Bury, he chased a through ball from team-mate Len Ashurst and as he approached the goal, he collided with keeper Chris Harker, resulting in him sustaining a tear to both the anterior cruciate and medial ligaments. Despite a brave attempt to return to full fitness, which included three months in plaster and a further 18 months of rehabilitation, he could only manage three further games before sadly announcing his retirement at the age of 29. The treatment for this injury has changed dramatically since those days and we would now expect to get a player back to full fitness. During the early 1980s the tide was changing and players started to recover and return to professional football, mainly due to the pioneering arthroscopic surgeon in Cambridge, David Dandy. To the best of my knowledge, Ipswich Town defender George Burley was the first player to recover fully from this injury and return to football. In my opinion it is no coincidence that Mr Dandy performed his operation. At the time there were various techniques to repair the ACL such as synthetic grafts, donor grafts and hamstring tendons. However, Mr Dandy preferred to use the patellar tendon graft as it was a living tissue from the player and had little chance of rejection.

Over the years I have been responsible for several players' rehabilitation from an ACL reconstruction. The first one was a couple of years after joining Luton. Our talented young defender Rob Johnson had sustained the injury so I took him to see Mr Dandy, who agreed to operate on him the following day. As ever, I asked if I could attend the operation, although I did so with not much hope as Mr Dandy was known for not letting anybody watch. To my amazement he kindly agreed, so the next day I watched in awe as this superb consultant repaired Rob's knee. It was a privilege and honour to see him at work.

The operation was a success but at the time there was little known about the rehabilitation, so I was tasked with devising a suitable protocol and exercise programme. It was a massive learning curve but I was extremely proud that Rob made a full recovery. However, to my horror he sustained the same injury when falling awkwardly in a friendly, this time to his other knee. Once again, after much hard work he made a full recovery and returned to enjoy a long and successful career.

It is sometimes easy to forget that these great surgeons are just normal people. I remember one occasion when I attended an operation on one of my players in Cambridge by the much respected and trusted Bernard Meggitt. It was a tight schedule as the operation started in the afternoon and we had a match at Kenilworth Road at 7.45pm. As ever I was welcomed into the operating theatre to watch, which enabled me to understand exactly how Mr Meggitt repaired the injury. The surgery had gone as planned but time was getting on and I would have to go straight to the ground without getting anything to eat. Mr Meggitt kindly said, 'I live nearby, come home with me and I will make you a sandwich and a cup of tea.' It was a simple and extremely kind gesture that I have never forgotten, but it did feel strange watching him make me dinner shortly after his hands were inside my player's leg.

These experiences with some of the greatest surgeons in the country are a long way from some memories I have from my early days in non-league football. When I started in senior football, I was amazed to see the warm-up consisting of a cigarette and a few stretches in the dressing room. I felt strongly about players warming up properly before a game, which at first was met with some derision and mickey-taking as I took them on the pitch – and from supporters too. Some of the players felt it would drain their energy for the game, but such was my passion and belief that this would enhance their performance, I would sometimes threaten them with, 'No warm-up then no game.' The players soon realised the benefits and noticed they suffered fewer injuries and often caught the opposition cold from the kick-off.

When I joined Luton, I also realised that warm-ups weren't even commonplace in professional football but over the years this changed. In modern-day football the warm-up is an integral part of training and matchdays and is planned and undertaken in a methodical manner by sports scientists, but it was the pioneers all those years ago who made it the norm.

When you are starting out in a career it is always nice to receive some praise to boost your confidence, and one such instance came while I was physio at Tring Town. We were playing against Watford at Vicarage Road in the Hertfordshire Senior Cup Final in 1978. Watford had just been crowned champions of the old Fourth Division. Graham Taylor wanted no slip-ups and paid us the highest compliment by picking almost their first-choice team. There was a close link between the two sides as a couple of directors were on the board of both clubs. Watford's chairman was a certain Elton John, who I recall coming down to sing and play the piano in the Tring bar after one home game.

At the time we had a very strong side and even though they were clear favourites we were quietly confident. The game was a hard-fought battle and at full time the score was 1-1, and with both teams wanting to win in extra time there were some strong challenges between the players. As a result of a bad tackle one of our midfielders sustained a nasty knee injury, and after assessing him on the pitch I realised it was serious so I made sure he was stretchered off into the dressing room. As I returned to examine him after the game, he was in a lot of pain so I reassured him while carrying out my examination. When I had almost finished, I heard a voice behind say, 'Can I help you?' Startled, I turned around and instantly recognised the man who had spoken to me – Dr Vernon Edwards, the quietly spoken Watford and England doctor. He asked what I had found during the examination, so I replied, 'He has a complete rupture of the medial collateral ligament and also damaged the ACL and medial meniscus.'

He then examined the player and after doing so turned to me and said, 'What are you doing?' I wondered to myself what I had done wrong. He then continued, 'Why are you with Tring Town? You should be in the Football League. I watched you examine the player and you did a great job, not only reassuring him but also an excellent examination that I would have been proud of.' This was such a lovely gesture from a kind gentleman who served the England team for many years. The following season, his words became reality as I entered the Football League with their arch rivals.

However, not all of my experiences at Tring were as successful. Our home ground was called Cow Lane, which I believe had strong links with the late Horse of the Year commentator Dorian Williams, a nice man with an unmistakeable voice. Whenever we played at home my eldest son Andy, who was a nipper at the time, would come along to the game with me. I remember a few occasions when I had to run on to the pitch to treat a player and the crowd would start to laugh, so I would look behind me to see what was so funny only to see Andy appear and bend down to help me! One particular occasion sticks in my mind, on a freezing cold January afternoon. I had gone on with my medical bag and bucket of antiseptic water, and as I grabbed the sponge to treat the injured player's thigh the sponge had ice crystals on it and to my horror it turned bright red along with his leg. As I had applied it to his thigh it had inflicted several small cuts. Luckily no damage was done and the player soon jumped up and carried on playing, but Andy thought his dad was a magician as with one swipe of his sponge he could turn a player's leg red!

One of the worst places for a player to get hit with the ball is the testicles. While on the course at Lilleshall, I had learned the best way to treat this particularly painful injury is with the use of warm water on a sponge. This helps prevent any retention of urine and relieves discomfort due to relaxation of the lower abdominal muscles[1]. So, on my way to a Tring game I stopped at a shop and bought a little flask, which I filled up with hot water just in case anyone was unlucky enough to get a ball in their privates. Early on in the game our striker went down in agony as he was felled by a ball that hit him in that area. As I got to him, I pulled out the flask and sponge but unfortunately it was still a bit too hot. As he put it down his shorts he suddenly jumped up with a loud scream and shouted 'You bastard, you have just burnt my manhood.' Luckily, he didn't sustain any permanent damage, he is still a good friend, and has a lovely family!

My first spell at Luton definitely honed my knowledge and skills as a physiotherapist. With the help of Dr Berry, we built a medical department at the club that we were extremely proud of. The supporters were fantastic and realised that to have a successful team on the pitch the players needed to be fit. Therefore, the Bobbers Club kindly raised funds to help us buy state-of-the-art medical equipment which allowed the players to have the best treatment available. One of the most memorable pieces of equipment I bought during this spell was a brand new flotation tank. After much research I decided to buy a Delta Tank, which was used by the American air force to help their pilots relax and reduce stress. I was excited to take

---

1   This method of treatment was correct at the time, but over the years it has evolved and currently the correct way to treat a blow to the testicles is cold pack and light compressive shorts to give support. As always, if in doubt a medical practitioner's advice must be sought in case there is an underlying problem.

delivery and couldn't wait to introduce it to the players, and from day one they loved it as it helped them decrease pain, take away muscular tension and reduce any anxieties. Our Delta Tank was approximately 8ft long by 5ft wide and 4ft high, so big enough not to feel claustrophobic, and it had the Luton Town badge proudly displayed on the side. It held about 10in of water, which was saturated with 850lb of Epsom salt, which created a solution more buoyant than the Dead Sea. The warmth of the water was kept at the average skin temperature (93.5°F), and as it was soundproof and completely dark the players would often fall into a deep sleep.

One of our players, the skilful forward Godfrey Ingram, who went on to forge a very successful career in America, constantly used the tank. One day after training he asked me if he could use it but only for a short time as he had an important appointment that afternoon, so I said yes and carried on treating the other players. A while later, after all the lads had drifted off home, I cleaned the treatment room, locked up and headed off to my car. As I pulled out of the car park I realised Godfrey was still in the tank, most probably shrivelled up like a prune!

After turning the car around, I quickly headed back to the treatment room to make sure he was okay. We had the deluxe model that allowed you to play music through the internal speakers. So I started playing the Marianne Faithfull hit 'What's the Hurry' and with that Godfrey slowly woke up feeling relaxed. I said, 'Godfrey, I have got some good news and bad news for you. The good news is you have been in a deep sleep but the bad news is your appointment was three hours ago!' He took it in good spirits and I didn't have the heart to tell him he almost spent a night in the floatation tank.

News of our tank quickly spread and I was asked by the BBC if they could record a programme about it. The well-known presenter Paul Heiney came along to the ground to see me; he couldn't wait to try the tank and experience the sensation of floating. I believe the programme was well received by the Radio 4 listeners. Floatation tanks are still widely used today by people such as athletes, business people, the elderly and people with certain medical conditions. I am not sure if football clubs still use them but for us back then it was a sound investment and I think we were one of the first clubs in this country to use one.

* * *

David Moss – Luton Town 1978–85

I had been suffering with lower stomach problems for several months and despite trying to manage with treatment and rest, as soon as I started training or playing the problem was still there. I remember going to see a Harley Street specialist in London and when myself and John came out of the premises, we were both very underwhelmed to say the least! Continue with the rest and treatment was not what I wanted to hear.

John then began to look at different options and I remember him showing me an article in *Shoot!* about an operation that had been performed on a Birmingham City striker called Mick Ferguson, for a similar injury. By now we were both willing to try anything, especially as I was beginning to fear that my career could be over. John made contact with Birmingham City and was introduced to their club consultant Mr Polyzoides, who agreed to meet us. We went to see him and his diagnosis was completed within about 60 seconds and he told us he would operate and arranged for me to go into the Solihull BUPA Hospital where he performed the operation a few days after we had met him. Without knowing the technical details of the operation, he said it had been successful and he had also performed some more strengthening procedures in the area of the injury so that in time it would not return.

While I was in the hospital recovering, Mick Ferguson and BCFC goalkeeper Jim Blyth came to visit me which I thought was a lovely gesture. After a few days' rest it was back to work and slowly trying to work on getting my fitness back under the care of our brilliant physio John Sheridan. John excelled with his care and man-management of the players and when I finally was ready for a reserve team appearance, we were both a little bit nervous of what the outcome would be. Fortunately, it went well enough and although not 100 per cent pain-free at first it gradually became bearable and enabled me to get back playing first-team football. My comeback match was against Notts County, I scored and we won, so all in all it was a good day.

I know that without John's dedication and perseverance my career would probably have been over. Not only was John a brilliant physiotherapist but also a lovely human being and a friend for life.

5

Life at Luton in the 1980s

I CAN say with the utmost honesty that my first spell at Luton included the happiest times I enjoyed in professional football. I have supported the club all my life, from when I first went to watch them in the 1950s with my older brother Tommy, up until the present day. Working for them was a dream come true. I had the privilege to work with some fantastic staff and players throughout my time there, from the manager, coaches and office staff all the way through to Rene, our washing lady who always had a smile on her face.

The team had come a long way in a short space of time under the management of David Pleat and had gained a reputation for playing a bold and attractive brand of football. After just missing out on promotion in the 1980/81 season, we came back the next year with an underlying confidence and belief that enabled us to win the title at a canter. I hoped I played a small part in this success by keeping the players fit, allowing the manager to pick from a full-strength squad almost every week. We had a great group of experienced players which helped the younger lads develop. One of the most vital ingredients that these players possessed was a relentless will to win and they hated losing, which I believe was an essential quality for the success we enjoyed.

This quality held us in good stead for arguably one of the most famous matches in Luton's history. We had adapted quite well in our first year in the old First Division, but towards the end of the season a few results had gone against us and we found ourselves in the bottom three and in real danger of relegation as we travelled to Maine Road to face Manchester City in our last game. The only way to ensure our safety was to beat City, which would then send them down, while any other result meant we would head straight back to the second tier. I will remember this weekend for the rest of my life as it is indelibly imprinted in my mind. We met at Kenilworth Road on the Friday morning in preparation to travel to Manchester. As the players were getting on the coach, I noticed a quiet confidence and steely determination that they were going to fight for the club until the end. We had improved as a team and I couldn't believe there was a chance we would fall at the final hurdle.

During the Christmas period one of our main strikers, Brian Stein, had fractured his fifth metatarsal against Manchester City. This fracture can be troublesome due to poor blood supply to the affected portion of the bone. Brian was a fantastic player and a big loss for us in the fight against relegation. In the months that followed I had worked round the clock to get him fit and Brian was determined to play some part in the final game. David Pleat would always trust my judgement when deciding if a player was fit to play. On the morning of the match he asked me if Brian would be okay, so I said, 'His foot will be fine but he will tire near the end.' We needed him back, so it was a great boost for the other players, staff and fans that Brian was able to take his place in the starting 11 for the first time since he picked his injury up.

Before the game there was a calm atmosphere in our camp. I truly believed we would get the win that was needed to secure safety, especially with players of the calibre of Kirk Stephens, our inspirational captain Brian Horton, and Mal Donaghy in our team. Mal was a quietly spoken Northern Ireland international who you would definitely want in the trenches alongside you.

The match wasn't for the faint-hearted in front of almost 43,000 passionate fans crammed into Maine Road. David Pleat picked the team and tactics extremely well, and instead of being gung-ho and surging forward at every opportunity we remained patient. The first half was a tight affair but we came out for the second half with renewed optimism as we knew we were the better team. Whenever called upon the back four of Kirk, Clive Goodyear, Paul Elliott and Wayne Turner defended for their lives and restricted City to hardly any serious attempts at goal. Paul Walsh almost scored for us in the 62nd minute but was denied by a great reflex save. The lads continued to push for the winner and ten minutes later a great marauding run by Kirk down the right resulted in him hitting a ferocious shot that was saved by the keeper before deflecting back off the post.

With the end of the match fast approaching and the score still at 0-0, was it going to be one of those days? David was nervous and at one point his head was in his hands, so after taking a puff on my pipe I turned to him and said, 'I think we are going to win.' He replied, 'Are you sure?' so I said yes, even if it was just to pacify him! There were only five minutes to go when after a short spell of City pressure, our centre-forward Trevor Aylott cleverly found Brian Stein on the right wing. Brian's first attempt at a cross was blocked but rebounded back out to him, and somehow under extreme pressure he managed to get the second cross into the box. It beat the first man but Alex Williams, the City goalkeeper, cleared the danger with a flying punch to the edge of the area. The ball went straight to the magnificent Raddy Antic who showed fantastic ability as he volleyed into the bottom corner to score the famous goal that secured a dramatic victory and our First Division status.

We saw out the last few nervy minutes with relative ease. As the final whistle went emotions were high, and I remember David running on to the pitch to start his famous jig closely followed by me in my bright orange jacket! As we celebrated on the turf of Maine Road, it quickly became apparent we weren't the only ones on there as a large number of disgruntled Manchester City fans had invaded the pitch. Myself and our young centre-half Paul Elliott quickly became surrounded and I feared the worst. Paul calmly said, 'Stay with me, John, and I will look after you.' I replied, 'Thanks Paul, but I think we might need Superman.' All of a sudden a policeman on his horse appeared and escorted us back to the safety of the tunnel.

The emotion of the last nine months and at securing our place in the First Division in such dramatic circumstances meant there was a lot of relief and tears in the dressing room after the game. I must say that the Manchester City manager John Benson, his staff and players were magnanimous in defeat, which was a credit to themselves and their club.

Even though we didn't leave the ground for a long while after the final whistle there was still a large number of unhappy City fans gathered outside. They were emotional and upset after being relegated for the first time since 1966. The policeman on board our coach advised everyone to stay below window level, which was a great suggestion as the coach was attacked with stones and other missiles.

After a few hundred yards we unexpectedly stopped sharply and as I peered cautiously out of the window to see what had caused the delay, I noticed someone lying next to us on the road. Natural instinct took over so I got up, told the driver to open the door, then rushed down the steps to help him. It became apparent that while attacking our coach he had been hit by a car. As I started to administer first aid, the injured fan gave me non-stop abuse and spat at me, but undeterred I continued to make sure he was okay. Some other City supporters gathered around me and were growing restless. At that point I was told in no uncertain terms by a tough Mancunian policeman, 'For your own safety get on the f*****g bus, now.' The injured fan was safe and not in any danger, so I quickly took his advice.

When we finally made it out of Manchester the party started in earnest on the coach with plenty of champagne and beer flowing. Travelling back on the motorway it was great to see cars tooting their horns and flying scarves out of their windows. The coach got back into Luton just before midnight, and most of us made a beeline to the Ronelles nightclub in Mill Street where we celebrated long into the night. I remember getting home just as the milkman appeared in our road.

Another memorable game that springs to mind is from earlier the same season. On Saturday, 11 September 1982 we travelled to play the mighty Liverpool for the first time in almost eight years. They were the reigning First Division champions and had been the dominant team in both England and Europe since the early 1970s. After winning promotion the previous season this match was the one we were all looking forward to. Myself and many of the squad hadn't been to Anfield before and as we made the long trip north there was a feeling of both excitement and also a small amount of trepidation.

On a beautiful, sunny afternoon, the match kicked off and we came under immediate pressure from the star-studded Liverpool team. However, we held firm and in the 27th minute we managed to take the lead with our first meaningful attack. Brian Stein played a great through ball to our skilful forward Paul Walsh. Walshy then turned the talented Liverpool defender Mark Lawrenson inside out before playing a measured pass back to Steiny who placed his shot past Bruce Grobbelaar and into the corner of the net. However, the lead only lasted for five minutes after Graeme Souness equalised with a splendid volley from the edge of the area.

Disaster struck in the 37th minute when the diminutive Liverpool midfielder Sammy Lee played a speculative cross into our box and Jake Findlay caught the ball with ease. After throwing the ball out to Kirk Stephens, Jake immediately collapsed on to the floor holding his midriff, in a lot of discomfort. As soon as I got to him I realised that his diaphragm was in spasm and he was struggling to breathe. After stabilising him I took the decision to take Jake off due to the seriousness of his condition. This was the era before goalkeeper subs, so midfielder Raddy Antic came on as a replacement. Right-back Kirk Stephens was brave enough to volunteer to go in goal, but as part of my initial treatment I had to cut Jake's shirt. As we didn't have another one the Liverpool kit man kindly found a spare for us to borrow. Kirk did well for the remaining few minutes of the half but just before the break we conceded a goal to Ian Rush. A few years later, Kirk told me that the fans on the Kop were singing to him, 'There's only one Shakin' Stephens!'

During the half-time break, David Pleat decided to have a slight reshuffle of the team. Kirk swapped with Mal Donaghy who became our third goalkeeper of the day. In fact, Mal started his career in goal as a youngster with an Irish non-league team called St Agnes before becoming an outfield player. I don't think he would have dreamt all those years ago that he would end up playing in goal at Anfield facing the league champions. He was still a useful goalkeeper and was covering for Jake for the second time in a couple of years, having played for almost all of the game in goal as we won at Cambridge United. Mal was definitely reliving his youth as he walked out at Anfield for the second half and decided to play without gloves.

We restarted the game with renewed confidence and were rewarded in the 51st minute as David Moss ran on to an exquisite pass from Raddy to equalise with a superb finish from 20 yards. We continued to take the game to Liverpool and ten minutes later Mossy then turned provider. He broke from midfield and played a pinpoint pass forward to put Brian Stein in the clear. Brian cleverly took it round the goalkeeper to score his second of the game to give us a 3-2 lead. Liverpool were stung into action and began to apply pressure in search of a goal. They made a substitution and brought on the pacy Australian Craig Johnston to replace Kenny Dalglish. Despite everyone's best efforts, Liverpool eventually got it back to 3-3 when Johnston combined with Rush to beat Mal's despairing dive and score the equaliser from close range. There were a few half-chances for both teams during the final 15 minutes, but we were relieved to hear the referee's whistle to end the match and gain a creditable draw.

I thoroughly enjoyed my first visit to Anfield on what was certainly a busy but memorable afternoon. As I made my way up the tunnel towards the away team dressing room, Roy Evans and Ronnie Moran stopped me to invite myself and the Luton coaching staff into the famous boot room for a drink. To my mind it was an honour to be asked and was not an invite that was extended to all clubs. I remember sitting in there with Ronnie, Joe Fagan, Roy Evans, the great Bob Paisley and some ex-players. Even though it had been a long day it was definitely a privilege to chat and mingle in this iconic setting with these footballing legends. To cap it off, as I was leaving the ground, Roy and Ronnie gave me a crate of Guinness to share with the lads on the coach ride home. In my opinion, this was the day the players and staff realised we could compete in the First Division and also showed the rest of the league we were going to be a force to be reckoned with.

Throughout my career I would always look forward to playing Liverpool at Anfield. It was definitely one of my favourite grounds, even when on the receiving end of some good-natured stick from the famous Kop. I was pleased to revisit the ground in 2006 when my youngest son Paul played in the FA Sunday Cup Final with St Josephs of Luton. It was certainly a different experience watching from the Kop than from the dugout.

One of my other favourite places to visit was West Ham's famous old Upton Park ground. The atmosphere would always be electric and intimidating, especially from the fans standing on the notorious Chicken Run terrace. Over the years, I enjoyed some great battles there while with both Luton and Spurs. Win, lose or draw, the staff would always look after us after the game. I especially enjoyed spending time with long-serving manager John Lyall, a lovely, kind and articulate man who sadly passed away in 2006. His right-hand man Mick McGiven and physio Rob Jenkins always provided great hospitality with a drink and a hot steak pie. I believe Rob has been associated with the club for over 50 years after following on from his dad Bill.

After a home game we also took great pride in ensuring the opposing teams and staff were looked after. Part of my pre-match preparation was to ensure the ice machine was fully stocked with beer. This was an integral part of the game and highlighted the mutual respect clubs had for each other. I am privileged to have met some of the greatest characters in our game and listened intently to their words of wisdom.

Nowadays most top-level clubs travel to away games in either aeroplanes or multi-million-pound coaches. Back in the 1970s and '80s it was a completely different story as clubs would have to hire a coach from a local company to take them on their travels. Luton were no different and I remember one occasion when we were due to play away at Aston Villa on a Tuesday night. We set off from Kenilworth Road nice and early on our short trip to the Midlands and David had organised for us to stop at Corley services on the M6 for a pre-match meal. We arrived there in good spirits and after a light bite to eat we moved into a private room for the manager to start his pre-match team talk. He was in full flow when suddenly there was a loud knock on the door and a distraught bus driver burst in before saying, 'The coach has broken down and won't start. I have phoned the depot and they can't get another one out to us in time to get you to Villa Park, but we will be able to pick you up afterwards.' We rushed out into the car park to see if we could get it going, but despite our best efforts it wasn't going to move anywhere fast.

Somebody then noticed a clapped-out hotel minibus so there was nothing else for it, and a few of the staff went to see the hotel manager. Luckily he wasn't an Aston Villa supporter and after much pleading he kindly agreed to let us use it. David said, 'John, you can drive it. Get all of the players in the back, then go like the clappers to Villa Park. As soon as you get there, go to see the referee and hand in the team sheet so we don't get fined.' The minibus seemed to creak and groan as the lads crammed in the back. We set off in the race against time and as I sped along the M6 the players were telling me to put my foot down and giving me some good-natured stick. Especially Jake Findlay, who was trying to put his joke plastic tongue in my ear as we were in the outside lane! Numerous supporters in their cars were giving us double takes when they realised their beloved Luton Town players were crammed into a hotel minibus that was falling to pieces.

The minibus somehow managed to get us to Villa Park. I drove towards the main gate and was stopped by the steward, then as I wound down the window he said, 'Who are you?' I replied, 'We are Luton Town; things aren't great at the moment and this is the only coach we could afford!' He gave me a double take before looking at the clapped-out minibus, and thankfully he believed me and let us into the ground.

After parking next to the flashy cars, we rushed into the dressing room but had no kit or boots, which were still a few miles back up the M6 in a fleet of taxis with David and the staff. I left the lads in the dressing room and went to see the referee with the team sheet; luckily we had arrived just in time to avoid the fine. He thanked me and then started to tell me the rules and protocols he expected from the staff on the touchline, which included the signal he would use to allow the physio on to the pitch. As we had just been promoted he had no idea who I was, so I told him I would go back to our dressing room and tell the physio not to enter the field of play until he received the signal. To my amazement he added, 'Don't worry, as I have heard he isn't very fast anyway!' I replied, 'Thanks, I've slowed down a bit but I was a good runner at school.' He started to laugh as he realised who I was.

After explaining our predicament to him, I then returned to the dressing room. Unfortunately there was still no sign of the kit, but the players were well disciplined and even though they were in various stages of undress, most had started their stretching and pre-match routine. David Pleat and the kit arrived late on so the players managed to get changed extremely quickly and out on to the pitch just before kick-off, but understandably due to the poor preparations we were well beaten. After everything we had been through to get to the game it was no surprise, but as always, the lads gave their all.

This was a memorable trip to Villa Park but I will never forget another visit a couple of years later, this time for totally different reasons. We had enjoyed our best run in the FA Cup for a long time and our reward was a semi-final against high-flying Everton. They were enjoying a great season and were on course for their first league title since 1970. Although we travelled to Villa Park as underdogs, the players and staff were quietly confident. The lads played magnificently and weren't overawed in the slightest. We played some great football and, in my opinion, deservedly took the lead in the 38th minute from a truly wonderful right-footed strike from Ricky Hill that flew past Everton goalkeeper Neville Southall and into the top corner.

The score stayed the same until deep into the second half. We were close to pulling off a major shock but with just five minutes to go Kevin Sheedy equalised as his free kick crept past Les Sealey's despairing dive. Derek Mountfield, the big and commanding Everton central defender, then broke our hearts when he headed the winner in the second half of extra time. We hunted for an equaliser but to no avail, then the final whistle went and the emotion of the last 120 minutes hit us hard. Everyone was devastated and there were plenty of tears from the staff, players and fans. This was without doubt one of the most disappointing days that I have ever experienced in football.

The following morning, I went to Kenilworth Road to treat the injured players, David Pleat popped in and said, 'John, how did we lose that game?' I replied, 'I have no idea. I really thought we were going to Wembley.' Upon reflection I truly believe that over time football evens itself out and I was lucky enough to get to Wembley with Tottenham in 1987 and 1991, but I would have loved to have gone that year with such a magnificent group of players.

In my opinion David's knowledge of both league and non-league football was second to none. He would constantly be searching for players to see if he could pick up a bargain buy. As a club we didn't have a lot of money so his talent for spotting a hidden gem paid dividends. He discovered some fantastic players from the lower leagues including Brian Stein from Edgware Town, Mal Donaghy from Larne and Emeka Nwajiobi from Dulwich Hamlet, and he spotted Ricky Hill playing for John Kelly Boys Technical College. Another way of unearthing a top professional for a reasonable price was to buy players who were injured and then it would be down to me to get them fit. However, before we ever parted with any money David would ask me to research them and decide if I could get him back playing. This was the era before the internet, so I would check the Rothmans yearbooks to see how many games they had played during the previous seasons and also speak to the physios of their present and previous clubs to get an insight into their history and personality. This method of recruitment allowed David and the club to uncover some real finds and several went on to become legends at the club.

Unfortunately, sometimes when I researched a player, I discovered they were either unlucky with injuries or had a serious problem. On one occasion David came to see me and said, 'We have a chance of signing an ex-international defender, can you look into his history?' Out came the Rothmans yearbook and I discovered that he hadn't played many matches at all in the previous few years. I continued my research and discovered that he had a serious persistent knee injury and, in my opinion, it was unlikely that he would be able to play many more games. David phoned me in the treatment room and said, 'Another club wants him, so we need to move fast to secure his signature.' I told him what I had discovered and that in my opinion it would be a mistake to sign him. He then put the phone down on me and I assumed that was the end of the matter.

Five minutes later the phone rang again and he asked if I was sure. I replied, 'I can never be 100 per cent sure but in my opinion, you shouldn't sign him.' The next day David said to me, 'We lost out on a good player and now he has signed for someone else.' I started to question myself but I was sure it was the right decision. A couple of months later my fears became a reality when David came to see me and said quietly, 'You were right about him.' Unfortunately after only a handful of games for his new club he was forced to retire. On this occasion I would have loved to have been wrong and endure the manager's wrath.

Throughout my career I have prided myself on always putting the health and wellbeing of a player before football, but this can sometimes come back to bite you. In 1984 we signed an ex-international player on a month's loan with a view to a permanent deal. His loan coincided with a short break to Kuwait to play a friendly against their national team. This player played the whole game then we returned to the hotel and after a good night's sleep, I went down for breakfast the next morning. He was also an early riser and had got up at a similar time, but as I followed him to the restaurant I noticed he was limping worse than me. We shared a table together and started to chat away about his injury problems. I was honest with him and said, 'I know you are struggling, but unfortunately I can't recommend the club signing you. You have to think about your welfare. I know you have enjoyed a fantastic career at the pinnacle of the game and with your track record and knowledge, you could become a great coach especially if you stop playing sooner rather than later.' Deep down I think he realised his career was coming to an end. I advised him what I considered would be the best way to speak to his club and medical staff if he decided to take my advice. He promised he would go away and think about it.

At the end of his loan he went back to his club and nothing more was heard until a few weeks later a livid David Pleat came to see me and said, 'John, his club are going to sue you, why did you tell him to stop playing?' I replied, 'David, I am more than happy to stand up in court and admit that I advised him to retire. I was only protecting him while he was under my care.' Nothing came of the threat but I was pleased to discover that he took my advice and decided to retire, and he went on to become a fine coach and manager at the highest level. Years later I was told he had written in his autobiography that the care and advice he received at Luton helped him continue his career in professional football.

* * *

Brian Stein – Luton Town 1977–88

Myself and Martyn Sperrin signed for Luton Town from non-league Edgware Town in October 1977. At the same time my older brother Edwin also joined on a month's trial. David Pleat became the new manager in 1978 after Harry Haslam had left the club to take over at Sheffield United. When John joined in 1979, I immediately realised how good David was at spotting top-class physiotherapists, as John turned out to be the best one I've ever played for. The lads in the dressing room always had absolute trust and faith in him and appreciated his kindness, honesty and integrity. John placed our wellbeing and health before football and I trusted him completely. He would constantly tell me I was too brave for my own good, so to help protect me I had to promise to tell him whenever I felt an injury.

During our first year in the First Division in the 1982/83 season, we played Manchester City at Kenilworth Road on 11 December. I scored a goal in an impressive 3-1 win, but during the first half I received a knock on my right foot. At half-time John had a look and placed my foot in an ice bucket to help stop the swelling. I managed to get through the remainder of the match but afterwards I went to hospital to get it checked. An x-ray showed that I had sustained a fracture to the fifth metatarsal, so to help aid recovery I underwent an operation to my right foot. For a few weeks I had to stay at home and keep my foot raised. I felt frustrated as all I could do was limp about the house. It seemed to take ages to heal but as soon as the plaster came off, I was desperate to get back playing.

During this time, I felt detached from the players as I was not involved with them for quite a while and I didn't realise what they were going through. John told me to be cautious but, in my desperation to help the team I tried to run and turn too early. I regret it but I ignored John's advice. This was the first time I had done so and it was the last, as unfortunately I sustained a fracture on the callus that had formed around the original injury due to pushing myself too hard. I was absolutely gutted because two months after the initial injury I was back to square one. After a short spell in plaster, I was back in the medical room working with John from morning until night but this time I made sure I adhered to his schedule.

As we approached the end of the season the team were struggling in the league and in real danger of relegation. In our penultimate game on Monday, 9 May, we were well beaten away at Manchester United. I was close to a return, so a couple of days after the game David Pleat arranged a friendly match against Watford to try and help me gain some match fitness as I had not played for over four months. I was so pleased to pull on the Luton shirt again, but the game against our arch rivals was anything but friendly and for whatever reason the Watford players were targeting my right foot. I managed to survive unscathed for 65 minutes when Pleaty decided to take me off for my own safety. After the game David asked me how I felt, I replied 'okay' but to be honest I had worked so hard to get back I was never not going to play against Manchester City. We had such a camaraderie at Luton and I wanted to help and wasn't going to let anyone down.

After training at Kenilworth Road on the Friday morning, we travelled to a hotel in Manchester to prepare for the next day's game. I was surprised that there wasn't a lot of banter on the coach as I think the players had lost their confidence. I was looking forward to the match and when we arrived at the ground the next day there were thousands of Manchester City fans spouting verbal abuse against us. It was a little bit scary but we just had to man up. Before the game Pleaty gave his team talk in the dressing room and told us to be sensible and not to go for it. He wanted us to stay in the game and not to concede any goals.

The game kicked off and the City players targeted me as they were trying to stamp on my foot but I was too quick for them. We set up in a 4-3-3 formation with Paul Walsh, Trevor Aylott and myself playing up front. On-loan Tony Godden was in goal, Basher [Kirk Stephens] at right-back, Paul Elliott and Clive Goodyear the centre-halves and Wayne Turner the left-back. Our three midfielders were Brian Horton, Ricky Hill and Mal Donaghy. We played okay in the first half. City seemed to be playing for a draw and sat back so at half-time it was still goalless. Halfway through the second half David decided to go for it, so he put Raddy Antic on for Wayne Turner. Not long before the final whistle I found myself on the right side of the penalty area, where I crossed the ball into the box and it was cleared straight back to me. I whipped the ball back into the six-yard area but the City keeper Alex Williams dived and punched it out of the penalty area. It ended up at the feet of Raddy who skilfully struck the ball like a bullet into the net past Alex. Immediately, 5,020 people went crazy as we took a giant step closer to survival. The next five minutes seemed the longest I have ever experienced as City pushed for an equaliser.

The final whistle eventually went and Raddy became an instant folk hero in Luton and in the dressing room. David Pleat danced his now-famous jig in celebration while the Manchester City fans invaded the pitch and confronted some of our players and staff. Myself, John, Paul Elliott and Mal Donaghy were assaulted, but we rightfully defended ourselves and eventually got back safely with the help of the police. Our dressing room was buzzing and all the lads were in tears of joy. I was shocked as I had not played for over four months and I had not suffered the pressure they had to endure. We were advised to stay in the dressing room longer than normal as their fans were waiting for us outside. Thankfully there was a lot of police at the ground and they tried their best to protect us.

The coach ride home was a lot different to the one up the previous day as the lads seemed to have got their mojos back and never stopped talking as we all partied back to Luton. I noticed John, Pleaty and the rest of the staff were so proud of what we had just achieved. It was a wonderful night and after getting back to the club around midnight, some of the lads still wanted to celebrate the victory so we ended up in the nightclub Ronelles in Luton.

John knew my family played an important part in my life and he was always welcoming when meeting them. My father Isaiah Stein would often pop into the physio's room. He was an incredible man who brought our family to England in January 1968 with my mum Lillian. They had brought seven children and left my elder sister in South Africa as she did not want to come to England. Both of his parents were priests; he was born in Durban and followed his brother to Cape Town in 1950. There is some thinking that says he was adopted by a Jewish family in Cape Town and took the name in order to beat the laws which had restricted his movement between different areas of Cape Town. Apartheid had been implemented in South Africa in 1948 and my father became a political activist. He was the first black South African to be put under 24-hour arrest. I know that he was imprisoned for political activism on more than three occasions, and during this time he had got to know Nelson Mandela.

The Archbishop of Canterbury met my father as we got off the boat at Southampton docks and the BBC were there to interview him. We took a train to London and went to a hotel and stayed there for a couple of weeks. My father met many British anti-apartheid campaigners and joined the South African Non-Racial Olympic Committee, which pursued a remit of organising against any country whose government would permit South African sports teams to play against them. I know that he was instrumental in the fight against apartheid in South Africa and getting Nelson Mandela out of prison. My father was not a man of violence and gave his life for the struggle, not just for black people but all people. He preached dialogue and believed ultimately that anything could be solved by talking. Dad was an amazing man and everyone he met could not help liking him.

After securing our status in the First Division we were already looking forward to the next season because we knew we had more to give. John and the staff had the players' utmost respect. We also had a great captain in Brian Horton who galvanised the team on the pitch, and David Pleat was a fantastic manager. After spending nearly five months with John during my return to fitness, I have to say I learned a lot about him. He is an incredible person, unbelievably kind, honest, trustworthy, hard-working and a great physiotherapist who knew his stuff but most importantly understood his players.

6

Off to Spurs

THERE HAD been rumours for a while that some of the so-called bigger clubs in England were interested in our manager David Pleat. This came as no surprise to me as over the past few years he had built a team at Luton that was admired for its attacking, exciting and enjoyable brand of football. I was preparing for a match near the end of the 1985/86 season when I first heard the news that he was going to leave. Assistant manager Trevor Hartley pulled me to one side and said, 'David has just told me he is going to become the new Tottenham Hotspur manager next season. He also said he wants me and you to go with him.'

I was shocked and my head was in a spin, not by the news of David leaving but because he wanted me to follow him to Spurs. At the time a physio moving to a new club with a manager was unheard of, so it certainly came as a surprise to me. Tottenham Hotspur were one of the biggest clubs in the country and steeped in history. Their team was full of household names and star-studded international players so it would be a step up, but I was confident in my ability. However, if the offer came it would not only affect me but my family as well.

The thought of leaving Luton had never crossed my mind. I was extremely happy at the club and over the past seven years had developed into a confident physiotherapist. Myself and Dr Berry had worked hard to improve the treatment room and it was now the envy of many of the bigger clubs, but more importantly I enjoyed a great relationship with the players, some of whom have become lifelong friends. However, my salary was still relatively low, and without win bonuses it was less than I earned while working at Whitbread in 1977. I even sometimes had to dig out my old tools and work as an engineer in the summer break to earn some extra money to enable me to take the family on holiday. The opportunity to improve the standard of living for my family was extremely appealing, but also the chance to test myself in the pressurised environment of a club challenging for domestic honours definitely interested me.

Shortly after the last game of the season, David came to see me. He confirmed that he was leaving and wanted to take myself and Trevor with him to Tottenham. During the conversation he promised that I would be on a much better package than at Luton with a large pay rise, a company car and good bonuses. It was a flattering offer but there was a lot to consider, and I was concerned the extra travelling and responsibilities would mean spending less time with my family. But after much soul-searching and many conversations with Betty, I decided to consider David's offer and speak to the Spurs chairman Irving Scholar.

A few days later I found myself travelling to Tottenham's famous old ground at White Hart Lane. To help make a good impression I bought a new whistle and flute (suit – I started to learn Cockney as I thought it might come in handy over the next few months), but unfortunately I didn't try it on before the meeting and the trousers kept trying to fall down as I had picked up the wrong size! Apart from that the meeting went well and the chairman gave the impression he was extremely keen for me to join, but there was still one big obstacle in front of me. Mike Varney had given Spurs years of loyal service as a physio and the thought of him being sacked didn't sit kindly with me, so I raised my concerns with Scholar. He assured me that Mike was going to leave anyway. I am unsure if this was actually true but to this day myself and Mike are good friends. After hearing this, I shook Scholar's hand and agreed to leave Luton to join the biggest club in north London. After returning home to share the news with Betty and the children, my next task was to inform Luton Town chairman David Evans of my intention to leave the club with David and Trevor. To say he was disappointed that the three of us were moving on was an understatement.

The transition from Luton to Spurs lasted for two weeks, which meant I looked after both sets of players over this period. There was no way I would have left my players at Luton in the lurch as they felt like family to me and to be honest it was still with a heavy heart that I was leaving. However, they were going to be in safe hands as the person to replace me was reserve team physio Dave Kirby. I had worked with Dave over the past few years and handed on my knowledge. He was keen, wanted to learn and was a very kind person who would do anything for the players. I felt he was the right man to move from his part-time role into the full-time position, so after the transition period finished my focus turned to Spurs.

On the first day at my new club I drove through the leafy lanes of Hertfordshire on the way to the training ground at Cheshunt. My thoughts turned to my beloved dad, looking down on me from Heaven. He is my guardian angel and I knew he would be proud of what I had achieved in my life so far. I felt nervous but excited as I entered the car park. Even though I was replacing an excellent physio, I was confident in my ability to do the job. My seven years at Luton had turned me from a man who was scared about entering professional football to someone who was assured that he would be able to perform at any level.

From day one the Spurs players were very welcoming. Football is a close-knit circle and I'm sure the players had talked to some of the Luton lads to get an insight into myself, David and Trevor. I had also inherited a full-time assistant; this was a first for me as at Luton we were only able to afford a part-time physio for reserve games. When I accepted the job I was offered the opportunity to bring in my own assistant, but as Cliff Speight was already in post the last thing I wanted to do was get him the sack.

One incident in the first few weeks showed the players the type of person I am. The England international and club legend Glenn Hoddle walked into the treatment room and politely asked if I would treat his knee. At the time I had two apprentices on the benches. It was early in the week and with no matches coming up, I said to him, 'Of course, Glenn. I will just finish looking after these two, if you want to pop and get a cup of tea and I will have a look at you in about 20 minutes.' So off Glenn went to get a drink and wandered in 20 minutes later, and as I was examining his knee he said, 'John, I don't normally have to wait for treatment.' I replied, 'Glenn, if it had been a couple of days before a game then that's different and I would prioritise. But I always try and treat all players the same and give everyone my utmost concentration, whoever it is.' Glenn then said, 'I am not complaining, John, I think it's brilliant and completely agree with you.' He was a pleasure to treat and would always say thank you, which meant a lot to me.

Before I joined Spurs, I was aware that Glenn had built up a trusting relationship with faith healer Eileen Drewery and would go to see her to help overcome his injuries. He asked me, 'What do you think about this type of healing?' I replied, 'I'm sure between Eileen and myself we can work together to keep you fit.' I met her on several occasions and I must say it was always a delightful experience.

I thoroughly enjoyed my first pre-season with the club. I felt comfortable in the new environment and had started to form a strong bond with the players. David and Trevor had made a good impression on the training pitch and we had a formidable squad for the upcoming season. There were a few new faces, including left-back Mitchell Thomas from our old club Luton Town for £275,000 and the no-nonsense central defender Richard Gough from Dundee United for £750,000.

On the morning of Saturday, 23 August 1986, I arrived at White Hart Lane to prepare for our first league game of the new season against Aston Villa at Villa Park. After treating a couple of players and packing the medical kit, it was time to board the brand new club coach for the journey to the Midlands. The entire squad and staff had been given a tailor-made blazer, grey trousers, white shirt and club tie and I felt immense pride to wear the famous Spurs cockerel on the breast pocket. As I sat down in the leather seats on the luxurious coach, I was surprised but delighted when a steward presented me with a menu and asked for my dinner order for the journey home. There was a buzz and sense of excitement on the coach as we travelled north along the motorway with a good squad and high expectations. Luckily we enjoyed a dream start and a dominant performance resulted in a 3-0 win, thanks to a hat-trick from Clive Allen.

As you can imagine the players were in good spirits on the journey home. The meal on the trip back to London was similar to dining at a top restaurant – the tables were laid, we had solid silver cutlery, three courses and unlimited drinks. I looked at David and Trevor and my mind went back to our time at Luton when after a match David would ask the driver to stop at the nearest fish and chip shop. This was the time of no mobile phones to pre-order food, so somebody would have to get off the coach and wait in the queue to order 20-odd fish suppers. We would then enjoy eating our dinner out of chip papers with a wooden fork and a can of beer. Suddenly the old days of clapped-out and rented coaches seemed a million miles away, but they were great times.

The 1986/87 season has gone down in history by many Tottenham supporters as one of their most memorable of the modern era. It had promised so much and we had been in serious contention for the First Division, FA Cup and League Cup, but unfortunately just fell short in all three of the competitions. However, my dream of going to Wembley had finally come true thanks to a convincing 4-1 win against Watford in the semi-final of the FA Cup thanks to two goals from Steve Hodge, one from Paul Allen and one from top scorer Clive Allen. Our reward was a place in the final against John Sillett's hard-working Coventry City side. The euphoria the staff and players felt at the final whistle helped overcome the bitter disappointment of the recent semi-final defeat at the hands of our arch rivals Arsenal in the League Cup.

Two weeks before the final, we travelled to the City Ground to play Nottingham Forest in the league. Just before kick-off I went on to the pitch to collect the players' tracksuit tops when all of a sudden, I felt someone give me a big hug from behind. To my surprise and astonishment, it was Brian Clough, who said, 'John, I am so pleased you are going to Wembley with David.' It was such a lovely gesture from a fantastic and thoughtful man. To be honest I was amazed he even knew who I was let alone my name, but looking back I must have stuck out like a sore thumb; I can't think of any other physios that ran on to the pitch with a limp. This proved to be true as over the next few years some of the great names in football would greet me with my first name.

Over the next couple of weeks the excitement continued to grow. It was a pleasure to be an integral part of the preparations for a major cup final. There were tickets for family and friends to organise, a team photo, a trip to Hummel for cup final clothing and the traditional cup final song had to be recorded. Luckily I didn't have to take part in the singing, but saying that there were plenty of the lads who fancied themselves as singers, especially Glenn Hoddle and Chris Waddle who released their famous single 'Diamond Lights' the same year.

The night before the final we stayed at the luxurious Ponsbourne Hotel in Hertfordshire. After enjoying a relaxing evening, I woke up the following morning with a sense of anticipation of what the day would bring. This was the era of when the FA Cup Final was the highlight of the sporting year, so as we left the hotel, we were surrounded by TV cameras and the eyes of the watching world. As the coach travelled along Wembley Way, I had to pinch myself that after all these years and against all odds I had finally achieved my dream of getting to a final at the world-famous stadium.

Just before kick-off, I walked up the tunnel and heard the cauldron of noise. My spine tingled and I hoped I would get the opportunity to run on to the hallowed turf. My chance came in the second half when Chris Waddle went down under a heavy challenge from Coventry midfielder Lloyd McGrath. So, in front of a capacity crowd of 96,000 fans and millions watching around the world, the limping physio ran on to the famous Wembley pitch. Luckily, Chris had gone down in the centre circle so I didn't have too far to go! While I was treating him, the BBC commentator John Motson paid me a lovely tribute, 'Just a word about the physiotherapist John Sheridan. He's a man well equipped to deal with injuries because John was disabled as a young man and he doesn't mind me saying so, he often gets a few good-natured cat-calls as he limps across the pitch because he had an accident at the age of 15 when he fell from the stairs of a bus and broke his hip and leg in three places.' After making sure Chris was okay, I ran off and the crowd started cheering. John continued, 'He won't mind that and gives them a little wave; it's a salutary lesson of what you can achieve in the face of adversity.' Even if I didn't get the chance to achieve anything else in football and after everything I had been through in my life, I was happy to fulfil my dream. We went into the final as firm favourites but unfortunately were beaten 3-2 in extra time by Coventry .

Even though I thoroughly enjoyed my first year at Spurs, I still sometimes asked myself if I had made the correct decision leaving Luton. The extra travelling from Bedfordshire to London seven days a week meant that the pastime I loved the most – spending time with my family – became less and less frequent, but thankfully they were understanding and extremely supportive. Even on the occasional day off it would be difficult to relax as the phone would never stop ringing. My youngest son Paul was, and still is, football-mad, and in his school holidays he would always ask if he could come with me to work and watch training. He loved doing that and got to know the players really well. I now look back and wonder how I managed to spend seven years at Spurs, but more importantly how did my family cope?

Despite the problem of not seeing my family enough, professionally I was extremely happy at Spurs apart from one issue that forced me to consider my future. Dr Brian Curtin joined Tottenham in 1962, becoming the chief medical officer four years later, and throughout his time at the club he had seen many physios come and go. Over the years he had formed strong relationships with many surgeons in London. However, while at Luton I had worked hard on building trusting relationships with other consultants and surgeons around the country and was determined to be loyal and keep using them for my injured players. This was a constant issue between the two of us and even though I was prepared to compromise, Dr Curtin stood firm and insisted we only use his consultants in London. It was a battle of wills between two strong personalities and there were many heated arguments as we both felt passionately about this issue. It wasn't the greatest start to our relationship and unbelievably I was told he actually phoned the Chartered Society of Physiotherapy to check my qualifications. After locking horns for months, we eventually came to an agreement to use a mixture of his consultants and mine.

Under that crusty, gruff veneer, which he displayed towards me at the beginning, there was a very nice, affable doctor with a vast knowledge of medicine. Over the next few years we grew close and went on to enjoy a trusting relationship, especially when he realised my priority was for the players' health and welfare with football coming a distant third. We both left the club in 1993 and kept in touch, and many years later I received a Christmas card from him which said 'Happy Christmas John, you were the best'. This message meant a lot to me as it proved that even though we had a difficult start, we became close friends and worked well together.

About a year before he sadly died, his wife Sue wrote to me saying that he was not well and asked if I would visit as he would love to see me again. I didn't hesitate to agree and after a long trip from my house in Corby to his home in a little village near Hertford, we spent a wonderful afternoon with a cup of coffee and a sandwich reminiscing about our time together at Spurs. His lovely wife did kindly write to me a short while after he passed away, thanking me for seeing him and saying that he had seemingly enjoyed it as much as I did. She also mentioned that he had not seen any one from the club for several years and that he was really happy to see me. This was very humbling to hear and I was so pleased that I had travelled to see him one last time.

An early snap of me. The hairstyle is still the same!

Aged 12 and enjoying fun times fishing in Rye

The infamous 650cc motorbike with sidecar that almost killed my passenger!!

Ten pin bowling title decider

Winning the title with the Cresta's ten pin bowling team

Betty and I on our wedding day. Over 50 years later we are still as in love as ever!

The successful St John's Ambulance team of myself, Eddie Edwards, Ken Rees and Rex Hayward

Great times with Taverners (end of back row)

Celebrating with Taverners manager Pete Wyder

Physio for the Bedfordshire County side (Back row – third from the left)

Receiving the highly coveted Sportsman Award

The Vauxhall team of the 70's

My first year at Lilleshall in 1973. (Second row - fourth from the left)

Press cutting from the local paper reporting my move into professional football

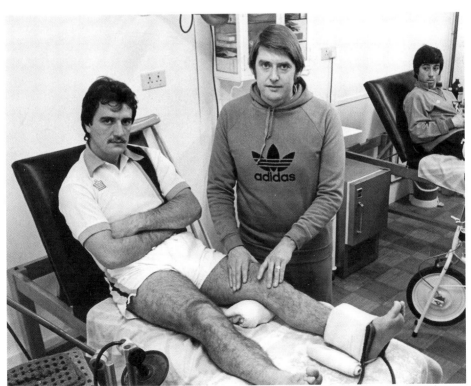

Treating Lil Fuccillo whilst Rob Johnson looks on

Carrying Mossy from the pitch with the help of Bob Hatton

Treating Luton Town legend Ricky Hill

Having a 'chat' with the referee whilst treating Brian Stein

Helping warm up Luton forward Trevor Aylott

Luton Town team photo 1980

Fancy dress with Brian Stein

Merry Christmas!!

Pre-match preparations with goalkeeper Jake Findlay

Treating Tim Breacker and Mick Harford in my hotel room

Looking thoughtful whilst enjoying the famous old pipe

A generous donation from the Bobbers Club, this kindly helped the club buy state of the art medical equipment

Strapping legendary Luton striker Brian Stein's ankle before a match at Kenilworth Road

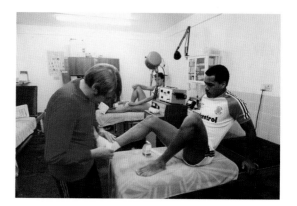

The backroom team with the Division Two championship trophy in 1982 (L to R - John Moore, myself, David Pleat, Trevor Hartley and David Coates)

An amazing day at Manchester City in 1983! (Shutterstock)

A great team, unlucky not to get to the FA Cup Final in 1985

My last team photo at Luton Town – 1985/86 season

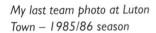

Tottenham team picture 1986/87

Treating Glenn Hoddle during my first season at the club (Shutterstock)

John Chiedozie looking cool!

Looking smart in my new Tottenham tracksuit!

A new manager for myself and the club

7

All Change at Spurs

DESPITE THE disappointment of finishing the previous year empty-handed, I truly believed that David Pleat had taken the team to a new level and we were all in a positive mood for the upcoming season. There had been a few changes in both the squad and facilities during the summer of 1987 as Glenn Hoddle and Tony Galvin had left, while the new arrivals included central defender Chris Fairclough and Dutch midfielder Johnny Metgod, both from Nottingham Forest. The training ground at Cheshunt had been sold for approximately £4m to be developed for housing, and while searching for a new training complex we had a short spell at Fergusons Sports Ground before finally moving to Chase Lodge in Mill Hill, which was owned by Camden Council. In the grounds stood a magnificent, Grade II-listed house from the early 19th century. Unfortunately, however much we tried, it was too small to accommodate a treatment room and gym as well as the changing rooms and offices that were required. Therefore it fell on my shoulders to find a solution.

During this period the club's purse strings were continually being tightened. It would be too expensive and time-consuming to build a new treatment room from scratch. I had to get creative, so after scouring the adverts in *Exchange & Mart*, Tottenham bought two old Portakabins directly from a North Sea oil rig. It was a far cry from the state-of-the-art medical facilities that are commonplace in today's football.

They arrived a couple of weeks later on the back of a low-loader lorry. The only place we could locate them was in a corner of the car park, about a two-minute walk from the main house. This meant there was no electricity or running water so to solve this issue I hired an old diesel generator to provide the power. Every morning when I arrived for work, my first task wasn't enjoying a cup of tea or reading the papers but instead trying to start the clapped-out generator. This wasn't as easy as it sounds, especially in the cold and frosty winter months. Occasionally it would run out of fuel and cut the power, so I would be unable to treat the players, but luckily I had my engineering experience to fall back on as I was forced to bleed the engine to get it running again. Each month when I ordered the medical supplies, I also had to order diesel and oil to keep the bloody thing going. After I left the club, I wondered how the job advertisement would read – 'Physiotherapist required, a knowledge of diesel engines would be an advantage'! The two Portakabins were linked by a corridor with the treatment room at the front and the gym at the back. Sometimes when you walked into the gym, I could imagine how it felt being in the North Sea with the smell of gas and extreme wind, especially after the lads had enjoyed a night out.

The season started well and by the start of October we were third in the league. However, rumours began circulating that chairman Irving Scholar wanted Terry Venables to take over from David as manager. After three successful years at Barcelona, Terry had just lost his job with the Catalan giants, the timing seeming to coincide with rumours of an issue in David's private life. All of the uncertainty seemed to affect the players and sadly the team suffered a dramatic loss of form. Due to Terry's availability and the pressure mounting on David for non-footballing reasons, he left his position at the end of October and Terry was appointed shortly afterwards. Unsurprisingly, he decided to bring in his number two from Barcelona, Allan Harris, who had been his trusted assistant for a number of years. This unfortunately meant Trevor Hartley also left, meaning I felt very vulnerable and wondered if I would be next.

David phoned me on the day the story of his issues outside of the game broke. He said, 'Don't believe what the tabloids have printed,' and asked if I could pop round his house to make sure his wife and children were okay. It was the least I could do but as I arrived, I was met by the sight of numerous tabloid photographers in his garden trying to get a picture of his family. I jumped out my car and told them to 'f**k off and get off his land or I will call the police'. One of them replied, 'We know who you are so you had better watch yourself as well.'

I remember David mentioning a couple of weeks earlier that he thought he was being followed. I strongly believe he was set up and nothing will ever change my mind, but unfortunately we will never know by who. A few days later, Irving Scholar called me to say I was not allowed to contact David. I was fuming and in no uncertain terms I replied, 'David is a friend of mine and I have no intention of not speaking to him. If you are not happy with this then you will have to sack me.' Luckily he didn't. To this day I have always stayed in contact with David and regard him as a true lifelong friend.

I drove to the training ground for my first meeting with Terry Venables still in a daze about what had happened over the last few weeks and wondering if my glorious time at Spurs was about to come to a premature end. He came over to see me in the treatment room, introduced himself and we enjoyed a brief chat about myself and the players. He then said, 'Have you spoken to David?' I replied, 'Yes I have, Terry, he is a friend and always will be. I haven't discussed what is going on at the club and never will. The only thing that interests me is looking after the players' welfare.' To my amazement Terry replied, 'Well done, John. I would not expect any less of you, how is he?' Just before Terry left to make his way to the training pitch, he checked the players' weights and said, 'These need to be recorded on a more regular basis; fat players are slow players.' I wondered what he would think of his new, slightly plump physio when he saw him running on to the pitch for the first time. I was quick out of the blocks but by the time I got to the injured player I was down to a fast walk!

To be fair to Terry, he could have quite easily sacked me on that first day. I was expecting him to bring in his own physio but he gave me a chance. I'm sure he did his homework and asked the staff and players their opinions as he is an astute man and if there was any doubt in my ability, he would have definitely got rid of me quite quickly. Over the next five or six years I never gave him less than 100 per cent but I can honestly say that our relationship wasn't always a bed of roses. Throughout my career I have always been my own man and would speak out if something wasn't right or needed improving. Maybe this affected his decision regarding not inviting me in to the England setup when he became manager in 1994. I was disappointed not to be included in his backroom staff as he never had any reason to doubt my loyalty and ability but for whatever reason it wasn't to be. I would have loved to have run on to the pitch as England physio just once and this is one regret I have from my time in football. If Spurs had stuck with David Pleat in 1987, I am sure he would have gone on to become England manager in 1990 and I would like to think he would have made me part of the national team's staff.

I immediately formed a good relationship with Terry's assistant Allan Harris, who was an extremely likeable man and had a great sense of humour. Shortly after Terry took over, he arranged for the players and staff to fly to Puerto Banús for a mid-season break. The trip coincided with an operation in Oslo on our Norwegian international goalkeeper Erik Thorstvedt. This was planned for a couple of days before the rest of the squad were due to fly back, so Erik and I travelled out there for a few days with the rest of the squad. As you can imagine, after everything that had gone on over the past couple of months, the lads were ready to let off a bit of steam.

Terry stayed in London so the responsibility to look after the players was entrusted to myself, Allan Harris and chief scout Ted Buxton. We stayed in a lovely hotel and as I was often first down for breakfast, I got to know the manager and staff really well. We were having a great time when suddenly the trip took a turn for the worse and, as they say, I had to 'take one for the team'. A day before I was due to fly to Oslo with Erik, some of the lads had become a bit boisterous and started to throw fruit and other objects from a balcony window at holidaymakers and staff around the pool. The matter had been reported to the hotel manager, who as you can imagine wasn't happy. I believe Allan was tasked with finding the culprits and bringing them to justice. Unfortunately for me, Allan had a brainwave! To avoid any further trouble or bad publicity he asked me if I would take the blame as I was leaving anyway. I wasn't too happy about it but could see the logic behind his idea, so to protect the players, I agreed to be the scapegoat.

The next day Allan went to see the hotel manager and said he had found the culprit and was going to send him home in disgrace, but when the manager discovered it was me, he couldn't believe it and didn't want me to leave. Undeterred, Allan told him that he wouldn't tolerate this behaviour and I would be sent home immediately. After packing I made my way to the hotel foyer to meet Erik and wait for our taxi to the airport. All of a sudden Allan appeared with the manager and started to give me an almighty bollocking. I don't know how we managed to keep straight faces and not give the game away. Allan was really getting into character, so much so that he even started to kick my suitcases down the steps, and the players were creased up with laughter as they watched from their balconies. It seemed to do the trick and I understand they enjoyed an incident-free end to their break; we certainly had a good laugh when Allan and the players returned from Puerto Banús.

Over the last few months Erik had been feeling pain and discomfort in his right knee while kicking a ball. We had been to see a consultant in London but the problem unfortunately persisted, so the next step was to visit the consultant to the Norway team, who was an expert in this field. After flying to Oslo we booked in to our hotel and enjoyed a lovely evening meal. The next morning, we met bright and early to catch a train to a small town called Moss, and when we arrived Erik had further tests which revealed a piece of sharp bone that had encroached into the patella tendon, causing the pain. After watching the operation and discussing the rehabilitation with the surgeon I had a shower and had a quick bite to eat, while Erik recovered from the epidural. The consultant gave him permission to leave hospital and fly to his home in Bergen, while I headed back to England. As we stepped out of the hospital doors we were greeted by the national media. My Norwegian isn't very good so Erik handled the questions and spoke to the press with his usual good manners and articulate way. Luckily one of the journalists offered us a lift to the airport, which saved us a lot of time and hassle. After a short summer rest Erik returned to the club to complete his recovery and was soon back playing in the first team.

Terry Venables becoming the new Tottenham manager was big news. I immediately noticed a difference around the training ground as the appearance of camera crews became a regular occurrence. Luckily they were usually there to film Terry at work, which meant I was normally left in peace in the treatment room. The profession we were in meant that appearing on film became part of the norm, but I preferred to stay out of the limelight and disappear into the background to concentrate on what I was good at.

However, I was once required to appear on screen. The cameras had been set up in Terry's office and my task was to walk in, act as normal as possible and give the manager an update on any injuries within the squad. The director told me it was imperative not to look at the camera as he wanted the shot to appear natural. I waited outside the office until I heard the camera man say 'come in', so I knocked on the door, walked in, smiled and looked straight down the camera and said, 'Morning boss.' 'Cut,' shouted the director. 'Remember to imagine the camera isn't here,' he added. I went out and tried again but for some reason as I walked in my attention was drawn to the camera. The other staff in the office were trying not to laugh but I could tell Terry was getting annoyed. There were two more attempts before he had seen enough and said, 'What we will do, John, if you go back to the treatment room and I will come in and ask you for the update, but whatever you do please don't look at the f*****g camera!' I headed back to the treatment room, followed by the television crew. After setting up the camera behind my back they eventually managed to get the footage they needed but I couldn't resist turning and smiling at the camera as Terry walked out!

Over the next two seasons we threatened to do well but without really achieving much. In the summer of 1989 the club made a marquee signing from Barcelona as England centre-forward Gary Lineker was brought in to form a fearsome attacking trio with Chris Waddle and Paul Gascoigne. There was much expectation from both players and fans alike that this could be the year that we seriously competed for domestic honours. However, a couple of weeks later Spurs received an unbelievable offer from Marseille for Chris and sadly he was sold for an amazing £4.5m. Despite this, the thought of Gary and Paul combining on the pitch was still a mouth-watering prospect. This was Terry's third season as manager and the team played well but fell short in the league as we finished in third place, 16 points behind Kenny Dalglish's formidable Liverpool side. Gary went on to have a great first season and finished as the First Division's top scorer with 24 goals.

Shortly before Gary signed, I discovered he was a great believer in oriental medicine so I attended an intensive acupuncture and shiatsu course at the College of Oriental Medicine in Sheffield. I have always been very open-minded about alternative medicine and found this course very helpful, so much so that I used many of the methods throughout the rest of my career and achieved some incredible results. However, one of these techniques almost got me in trouble with the manager – moxibustion, a form of heat therapy. It involves burning moxa, a stick made of mugwort leaves, on or near the body's acupuncture points, and I am reliably told it smells extremely similar to the aroma of cannabis. One morning Terry walked into the treatment room and immediately noticed the unusual odour in the air. 'Who the f**k is smoking that shit?' he said. Trying not to laugh, I had to reassure him that it was the medicine and not one of the players.

As well as learning about oriental medicine I was also lucky enough to enhance my knowledge of osteopathic medicine. One Saturday morning at the training ground in 1992, I was introduced to a clever man called Theo Peters. Theo was a tutor at the London College of Osteopathic Medicine in Marylebone. I immediately formed a good friendship with him as we shared a passion for medicine and rehabilitation. He invited me to attend his college on Friday afternoons to observe some of the most respected minds in medicine as they met each week to discuss unresolved and problem cases. At first he told me not to get too involved and just watch the doctors at work.

I took his advice and observed quietly for a few weeks; however, on one occasion a patient came in to the surgery with a knee problem. They discussed the treatment and prognosis when suddenly Theo turned to look at me and said, 'John is good with knees.' The man leading the meeting was a Canadian doctor called Douglas Longden, who was an expert in a new technique called strain and counterstrain. He beckoned me over to examine the patient and said, 'Mr Sheridan, the floor is yours.' I was a little bit nervous as some of the most knowledgeable doctors in the country were watching my every move. After speaking to the patient and getting his history, I conducted my examination of him and discovered the extent of the injury. I then turned to the audience and said, 'This man has suffered a badly torn meniscus [cartilage] which needs urgent surgery and unfortunately no amount of osteopathy will fix it.' I then explained how I had come to this diagnosis. Dr Longden said to the patient, 'Go and see your GP and tell him what John has found. I will write you a letter to explain our findings.' I think this really broke the ice with these guys and in return for allowing me to attend their college I was often asked if they could spend a few hours with me at the club, which I was always willing to do.

Theo was similar to myself in the sense that we were both open to different treatment concepts. He would occasionally come to watch me at work at the training ground where we would exchange ideas; I would show him traditional rehabilitation methods for sports injuries and he would demonstrate the strain and counterstrain technique. This new technique had positive results and I would often use it throughout the remainder of my career. It was a thoroughly enjoyable experience spending time with Theo and I'm sure I learnt a lot more from him than he did from me. He is a very talented doctor who went on to write many articles and a book on the technique of strain and counterstrain, which he asked me to read before it was published. Doing so was a great honour.

8

Paul Gascoigne and that Free Kick

THE NAME Paul Gascoigne still conjures up memories of a superbly talented Geordie footballer. Looking back just over 30 years later I feel the time is right to put pen to paper to say how he affected my life. The only reason I do this now is for my beloved grandchildren Jake, Sam, Lucy and Edward, as a couple of years ago they bought me a 'Dear Grandad' journal to fill in and wanted to know about my life and career in football.

For four years Paul was a big part of my life and no story of mine can be complete without sharing some recollections from this time. In a professional capacity he certainly kept me busy and I have many fond memories of him as a person. The next few chapters will explain our relationship from first meeting him at his medical, the build-up to the 1991 FA Cup semi-final and playing in the final of the same year against Nottingham Forest which left him fighting for his career and me for my sanity. Over the years I have been offered various amounts of money to talk about Paul and have always politely declined, but the opportunity to tell my grandchildren some of my experiences with him was too much to resist.

I first met Paul in July 1988; Terry Venables had asked me to organise a medical for a new signing the club was about to make. I called Dr Brian Curtin but he was on holiday at the time, although luckily his brother – who was also a doctor – agreed to travel to White Hart Lane to help with the examination. I also asked the highly regarded Harley Street surgeon John Browett to attend, which he kindly agreed to do. Medicals are a common occurrence over the summer months as historically clubs make lots of signings during this time. However, I was surprised to see Paul walk into White Hart Lane as I had read in the tabloids that he was due to sign for Manchester United. He arrived with two people – his dad John, who was a quiet and deep-thinking man and who I became friendly with during Paul's time at the club, and also his best mate back then, Jimmy 'Five Bellies' Gardner. I often look back and wonder if in hindsight he made the right decision coming south to delight the passionate Spurs supporters and enjoying the bright lights of London. I personally feel that it would have been more beneficial for him to stay closer to home under the care, guidance and discipline of Sir Alex Ferguson but unfortunately, we will never know. Despite the trials and tribulations Paul has suffered over the years, I still feel that he should be treated as one of the great British icons and become an ambassador for the Football Association and for football throughout the world.

I instantly found Paul to be a very likeable man with a depth of passion for football that I had rarely seen. His determination to work hard and improve was phenomenal. I would often see him after first-team training had finished, joining in with the youth team for extra practice. This commitment without doubt helped during his rehabilitation from the serious injuries he sustained over the next few years. He was also one of the most generous people you are ever likely to meet. There was one occasion when I invited a severely handicapped young Spurs supporter into the treatment room for a behind-the-scenes experience. He spent a lot of time with Paul and made some incredible memories. As I was about to give Paul some treatment, he said, 'I won't be a minute, John,' and ran out. About ten minutes later he burst back through the door with a wad of notes in his hand and gave it all to the young supporter to buy himself a present; a fantastic gesture. He would regularly attempt to give me expensive presents but I would politely decline as I felt that however close you got to some of the players, you had a duty to keep a professional relationship with them. One of the only things I would accept, however, was when a player would give me their match shirt as a thank you for getting them fit or looking after them over a prolonged period of time.

I feel that I can now give a different and unheard account of the injury that put Paul's career in jeopardy during a time when Tottenham's future was also in question due to serious financial troubles. Many books have been published alongside media documentaries but this is my personal account of the time when the football world waited with bated breath – would one of England's greatest players ever play again?

It all started when we beat Portsmouth 2-1 at Fratton Park in the fifth round of the FA Cup. We conceded first on a terrible sticky pitch but Paul won the game for us with two goals, the first a great header from a pinpoint Paul Allen cross and the second a fabulous individual effort that was worthy of winning any game. After the match he complained of discomfort and stiffness in both groins. The next round of the cup against Notts County at White Hart Lane was in three weeks' time, so with careful management we were able to keep him fit enough to play. Once again, he proved how important he was to the team as he scored the winner with a calm, side-footed finish from just inside the 18-yard box. However, after watching Paul during the game, I knew the injury was deteriorating rapidly and the time had come to make a decision on what if any part he would play in the remainder of the season. It was an easy call for me but I knew Terry wouldn't be happy as Paul had been the star player all season and was determined to get the club to the final. He was in a lot of discomfort and I knew what had to be done. So after he had showered, I spoke to Paul in private and explained what I wanted to do. As ever he was great and agreed 100 per cent to my plan as he knew that I would always make any decision for his best interest and wellbeing.

The semi-final was to take place at Wembley in four weeks' time and the average recovery period for this injury was five to six weeks. However, because of Paul's determination and work ethic and with a little bit of luck there could be an outside chance that he could play some part in that game. To be fair to Dr Curtin, he said, 'I will respect and support your decision, John.' Terry was more concerned about the semi-final and asked me, 'Can you get him fit in time?' I replied, 'I will try but I can't promise.' Disappointingly, my decision wasn't met with 100 per cent backing within the staff and I knew that it would be my head on the block if Paul wasn't back in time for the game.

The next morning myself and Paul went to Harley Street to see Mr Gilmore, who after performing his examination agreed with my diagnosis and advised urgent exploration and repair of his groin disruption. I attended the operation, which revealed that the decision to undergo surgery was correct as the injury was worse than first feared. In all likelihood he would have broken down completely, putting him out for the remainder of the season.

After four nights in Princess Grace Hospital, he went off to France for a week to rest and start a gradual rehabilitation programme. When Paul returned from his short break he was in good shape and as determined as ever. I continued to work round the clock with his recovery and it soon became apparent that there would be a good chance he would play some part in the upcoming game. His progress was astonishing and I felt pleased that the unpopular decision I made a few weeks earlier would be justified. Not long before the semi-final, Paul came to see me in the treatment room and said, 'Terry and Dave Butler want me to go away with Dave on a one-to-one basis to continue the rehab but I told them I'm going to stay at the training ground with John. He put his head on the block and he is the one that will get me fit.' I thanked Paul for his loyalty and nothing more was mentioned by either Terry or Dave. I quickly forgot what had just taken place as I had to focus on not just Gazza but also midfielder David Howells. He had recently undergone a meniscectomy, an operation for a torn meniscus, and was also battling to regain fitness for the big game against Arsenal. Both players were working hard and desperate to play against our arch rivals.

On the Monday before the Arsenal tie, Terry called me into his office for a meeting. He said, 'John, as you know we have a game on Wednesday, away at Norwich City. Do you think Paul can play some part?' I told Terry that he could play for a maximum of 60 minutes but then he must come off immediately to give him any chance of recovering for the semi-final. At this point in my Tottenham career I had moved into a consultant position, which meant Dave Butler ran on to the pitch and travelled to away matches with the first team. Due to the important nature of this game, Terry asked me to go to Norwich to keep an eye on Paul's progress. I agreed and travelled from my home in Luton to Carrow Road. After arriving at the ground, I immediately went into the dressing room and reiterated to Terry and Dave that however well Paul was playing they had to take him off after 60 minutes, no matter what. I made sure Gazza was okay before taking my seat in the main stand alongside my youngest son to watch the match.

In an under-strength side, Paul was named captain for the night. The first half kicked off and after a tentative start he began to ease himself slowly into the game. I was pleased to see that the longer the first half went on it was noticeable his confidence and fitness grew. The second half started and he immediately showed why he was regarded as one of the best players in the world as he began to spray pinpoint passes all over the pitch and beat opposition players with his strength and skill. This was the point I realised he was going to be fit enough to play some part in the upcoming semi-final. For the next 15 minutes he continued to run the game.

Sixty minutes came and went and it appeared from the stand that because Paul was playing so well there was a possibility he would stay on to finish the game. He was lacking in match fitness and if he had played much longer, he would be at risk of getting fatigued and picking up a strain which would most probably have ruled him out of the semi-final. So without hesitation I made my way down from the main stand to the dugout and asked Terry and Dave to substitute him without delay. During the next break in play his number was held up and I immediately took him to the dressing room to examine him. He was pleased to be back out on the pitch and said to me, 'John, I'm a bit stiff and tired but otherwise feel good.' The past few weeks had been hard work but I was delighted and relieved he came through the game unscathed. Another concern I had of leaving him on past the 60-minute mark was due to his lack of match fitness he could have quite easily sustained a different injury such as a muscle strain.

A couple of days before the semi-final I was summoned to Terry's office where he asked me my opinion about starting both Paul and David Howells. I told him, 'David will last the whole game as he did against Norwich and Paul will play 60 minutes before he starts to get tired.' Terry was delighted and after seeing how he had played in the first 15 minutes of the second half against Norwich, we both knew he could wreak havoc against Arsenal, especially as they would be unsure if he would be selected.

The night before the game at Wembley we stayed at the plush Royal Lancaster Hotel in London. After finishing our evening meal, I made sure all the players were okay and had settled down for the night. Before retiring to my own room, I decided to pop into the bar to enjoy a well-earned glass of red wine. After relaxing for a short while I decided it was time to go to bed as it was getting late. I went to get up out of the antique chair that I was sitting in and to my horror the arm fell off in my hand! Not thinking much of it, I decided to whack it back on and report it to reception in the morning.

The morning came and almost straight away I found myself extremely busy looking after the players. We had our pre-match meal and as Terry was about to start his team talk, we were interrupted by a knock on the door. In strolled the immaculately dressed hotel manager with an envelope in his hand. 'Is Mr Sheridan here?' he asked. After making myself known, he handed me the envelope. I told him I would open it later but he replied, 'Unfortunately, it is a serious matter sir and you need to open it immediately.'

To my horror everyone in the room was now looking in my direction. I quickly opened the envelope and gazed in astonishment as I discovered a bill of £280 for the repair of an antique chair. It slowly dawned on me that because it had been such a busy few hours, I had completely forgotten to report what happened the previous evening. I said to him quietly, 'I'm sorry but this is the wrong time and place. I will come over later and pay as I don't have that amount of money on me.' One of the players snatched the envelope from my hand and after reading it, said loudly, 'Who's been a naughty boy? Lads, we will have to have a whip-round for John as he broke a chair last night when he was pi**ed.' To my dismay, they got a hat out and started to collect some money for me. Luckily I was soon put out of my misery as the room erupted with laughter and it then dawned on me that they had set me up. Roy Reyland, our likeable kit man, had watched me whack the arm back on. To help try and calm the players' nerves before the game, he arranged with the hotel manager to interrupt the team talk and stitch me up. We did go out and win so it was a small price to pay for a great victory.

The semi-final couldn't have started any better as we blew Arsenal away in the first half an hour. Paul's brilliance was there for all to see as he scored a magnificent free kick from 35 yards in the fifth minute. It flew past David Seaman and into the top corner, then Gazza ran over to celebrate in front of the dugout. I felt so proud of him and what he had just done. After everything we had been through together during the past four weeks, I felt completely justified in the decision I made after the Notts County game.

Paul continued to influence the match and in the tenth minute we doubled our lead after he combined brilliantly with Paul Allen who then crossed into the Arsenal six-yard box where goal poacher Gary Lineker did what he does best and poked the ball over the line. The match finished in a memorable 3-1 win against our bitter rivals. After the game, I was delighted and emotional when both Paul and David paid me a great compliment by giving me their shirts as a thank you for what I had done to get them fit. Both of these shirts took pride of place on the wall in my private practice before I retired. I would often look at them and reminisce about what we went through in the build-up to one of the most memorable matches in the club's history.

9

That Tackle

SATURDAY, 18 May 1991 is a day that changed my life for all the wrong reasons. Over the next 12 months I encountered some of the most traumatic and stressful times I have ever experienced, many of which often had me fearing for my sanity.

On a beautiful spring morning I woke up at the Royal Lancaster Hotel. It promised to be a wonderful few hours as it was the day of our FA Cup Final against Nottingham Forest and also my wedding anniversary. My wife and family were going to join me at the hotel after the game and we were planning to enjoy a lovely long weekend, especially if we could win the cup. After his magnificent free kick in the semi-final, Paul Gascoigne had now fully recovered from his injury and was back to his best. With the talent we had in our squad such as Gary Lineker and our inspirational captain Gary Mabbutt we travelled on the coach to Wembley confident we were going the win the club's first major trophy since 1984.

Referee Roger Milford blew his whistle to start the match and after a cagey first few minutes the game burst into life when Gazza won the ball out on the right touchline. He uncharacteristically followed through with his foot and caught Garry Parker square in the chest. It was an outrageous tackle and deserved to be punished with at least a yellow card but amazingly Milford let him off with a warning. Paul was still pumped up when after 16 minutes he went in for another rash challenge, this time on the Forest full-back Gary Charles just outside our penalty area, and unfortunately this time both Paul and the team paid a heavy price. After the challenge he stayed down in obvious pain, so Dave Butler went on to examine him and following extensive treatment he gingerly got to his feet and took his place in the wall. Stuart Pearce then smashed home the subsequent free kick with such venom that goalkeeper Erik Thorstvedt could only watch it fly past him into the net to give Forest the lead.

From the restart Paul collapsed and fell to the floor as he tried to turn, and I immediately realised that something was seriously wrong. Dave ran back on to to treat him followed by me, and this time I examined him then my heart sank as I discovered that he had suffered a career-threatening injury. Paul had everything going for him – a dream transfer to Lazio, a swansong for Tottenham at Wembley and the possibility of becoming the best player in the world. This all seemed such a long way away as I walked alongside him from the pitch on a stretcher. When we got to the treatment room at Wembley, there was a moment when myself and Paul were alone and, he asked me, 'How long will I be out, John? Three weeks? Three months? Six months?' As I replied we both had tears in our eyes and I said, 'Let's wait until we see the consultant and have some tests but I fear it could be up to a year.' Throughout my career I have always cared about all of my players but after everything we had recently been through, I had developed a strong bond and friendship with Paul and this was to prove invaluable over the coming year.

While I tried to compose myself and gather my thoughts, the enormity of the situation hit me like a ton of bricks. Somehow we were going to have to beat the odds for Paul to ever play again, and Tottenham were relying on his transfer fee from Lazio to help the club survive as it had recently been reported they were up to £20m in debt. At that moment the door to the treatment room opened and in walked the club's consultant orthopaedic surgeon, John Browett, and our club doctor Brian Curtin. They asked me, 'How bad is it?' I ushered them towards the door so I could speak to them out of earshot of Paul. I told them what I had found and after John had examined him, he confirmed my diagnosis. There was an ambulance waiting to immediately transfer Paul to the Princess Grace Hospital for further tests. I started to get ready to go with him and asked Dr Curtin to make sure my clothes and belongings were taken back to the hotel. He replied, 'John, I don't want you to go to the hospital yet, you will be more valuable here in case we get another injury.' I knew Paul would be looked after so I decided to stay until the final whistle and then go straight to Princess Grace. Just before he was stretchered into the ambulance, I looked at him and said, 'Try not to worry. I promise I will look after you.' Paul nodded and knew they were not empty words.

The rest of the final became a bit of a blur as for the majority of time I was thinking of Paul lying in a hospital bed. However, I do remember Paul Stewart scoring from just inside the penalty box to take the game into extra time and then the own goal by Forest central defender Des Walker from a Nayim corner to hand us the win. After the final whistle went, it was fantastic to see Gary Mabbutt receive the FA Cup from the Duchess of Kent before turning and lifting the trophy towards the delirious Spurs supporters. However, it was sad to think that Paul wouldn't climb the famous steps of Wembley to get his medal as he had been our talisman in the competition and almost single-handedly got us to the final.

The day provided a real mix of emotions for me – from the despair of Paul's injury, to the elation of winning the FA Cup, to the reality of what was going to be a very difficult year. If I had known what was to come, I maybe could have prepared myself better as during Paul's rehabilitation I often felt alone and lacked some support from the club. Paul was big news and we were under constant scrutiny from not just Tottenham and Lazio but also the worldwide press. It was going to be a battle to save Paul's career in football and to also keep my reputation intact.

Upon returning to the hotel, the players and staff quite rightly enjoyed the post-match celebrations as it was a fantastic achievement for the club to finally win some silverware. The champagne began to flow but there was no way I could indulge as I would have to be up bright and early the following morning to attend Paul's operation. That evening I told Betty that unfortunately our anniversary celebrations were coming to a premature end, although the harsh reality of being married to a football club physiotherapist was nothing new to my understanding wife. Betty has always supported me and never complained as she accepted that the job was 24/7.

After lying awake half the night thinking about what the next day would bring, I arrived at the Princess Grace Hospital at 6am. I had a quick cup of tea before checking in on Paul who was understandably anxious but I reassured him that he would be okay. It was then off to meet John Browett and the rest of the theatre staff to discuss the operation. Just before having a shower and changing into the sterile theatre clothing, I thought of my wife and children who would just be leaving the hotel to go home and wished I was with them.

As we entered the theatre, I prayed the damage to his knee wouldn't be as bad as I first feared. John got to work and his initial examination showed a badly injured structure resulting in a complete rupture of the anterior cruciate ligament, a tear of the lateral meniscus and a quite marked tear in the medial collateral ligament and capsule. Due to the extent of the injury the operation took longer than planned, but by the time John had finished he had rebuilt Paul's knee with meticulous precision and deemed the operation a success. It now showed no signs of instability and I left the theatre with renewed hope that we could get Paul back fully fit and playing at the highest level.

After changing back into my clothes, one of the theatre staff kindly made me a cup of tea and I managed to grab a couple of biscuits to ease my hunger. Before heading home to Luton, I thanked John for all of his hard work and had a brief discussion regarding the start of Paul's rehabilitation. As I was about to slip out the back door, the hospital superintendent rushed up to me and said, 'John, you need to get a spokesman from the club to make a statement. There are hundreds of reporters and cameramen at the front door and it is affecting the rest of the hospital.' This was the last thing I needed as I was feeling extremely tired and just wanted to leave. Undeterred, I set about phoning the club to get an official statement about Paul's condition. After endless attempts to get through to someone at White Hart Lane, nobody answered and I realised the staff were quite rightly celebrating our cup win; the tradition of parading the FA Cup around London on an open-top bus was not going to stop for Paul Gascoigne.

While the staff and players were enjoying the rapturous cheers of the Spurs faithful, I sat down slowly by myself to prepare a statement for the waiting world. I carefully considered what would be the best thing to say in the interests of the club but more importantly for Paul. After writing a few words to say, I opened the front doors of the hospital at 12.30pm on that Sunday afternoon. Not for one moment did I expect the frenzy that hit me and after taking a short pause to compose myself I read the statement to the best of my ability. Afterwards I tried to make my way to the car but was hounded relentlessly by the media and cameramen. Luckily I knew some of them, so to defuse the situation I joked, 'Come on lads, you know I am not the fastest, you could have given me a head start!'

On the drive back along the M1 to Luton, my head was in a spin. I had just experienced the full force of Gazzamania and wondered what I had let myself in for. After finally reaching home, I was relieved to get back to the normality and safety of my family. That evening I settled down for an anniversary drink with my wife and to my amazement I looked at the TV and saw myself larger than life reading the statement on the nine o'clock news. It was easy to see that I looked tired but after everything that had happened in the last 24 hours it was no wonder.

To his credit, Terry Venables phoned me and thanked me for all I had done. He commented that I handled the situation well, looked calm and had done so with sensitivity. Even though I was on my own, I believed I managed to do the best for the player and also for the club. However, there was still a huge sense of sadness that I had not fully enjoyed the celebratory evening the night before and had also missed out on an open-top bus ride with the rest of the squad, which I would never experience. The thing that hurt the most and still does is that after everything we had been through during the FA Cup run that year, I have never received a winner's medal even though I had been promised one by the club. The only consolation is that I know in my heart I had done the right thing for all those concerned.

10

The Fightback Begins and Fishy Tales

IMMEDIATELY AFTER the operation, Paul's injured knee was placed in a continuous passive motion (CPM) machine. These are used in the first stage of rehabilitation to control post-operative pain, reduce inflammation and to protect the healing tissue. Every second was going to be important in his battle to return to fitness, so to be able to use this machine was definitely going to give us a great head start. Paul was in hospital for another 12 days and during this period the Princess Grace physiotherapist team commenced minor rehab. Due to this initial work, he left the hospital, able to partially weight-bear on his right leg. Myself and John Browett had already devised the next stage of his recovery, consisting of the knee being placed in a Donjoy brace which would provide support but also allow movement, and we anticipated he would be on crutches for three to four weeks. The long-term aim was for a return to playing in nine months when the patella tendon graft had become fully vascularised, which means the graft would be strong and have a good blood supply.

Due to Paul's moment of madness in the cup final his move from Tottenham to Lazio was in major doubt, so a meeting was set up between the two clubs to discuss the transfer and rehabilitation. After much negotiating it was agreed that if he could pass a stringent medical, Lazio were still prepared to take Paul from London to Rome. As part of the deal, the Italian club insisted that I would be responsible for his rehabilitation and within reason he couldn't go anywhere without me! There would also be regular updates between the two medical departments and periodic meetings would be held in both cities. Even though the spotlight would be on Paul, I also had four other players overcoming major surgery and they deserved the same amount of my time and dedication. I quickly realised that the next 12 months was going to be full-on.

The 1991/92 season saw major changes at the club. Terry Venables moved upstairs to become chief executive under the stewardship of new chairman Alan Sugar, while Peter Shreeves re-joined as first team manager. Although this was the first time I had the pleasure of working with Peter, we instantly formed a great relationship and I thoroughly enjoyed his wicked sense of humour. He was going to be ably assisted by Doug Livermore and Ray Clemence, who would make up the remainder of the coaching staff.

During the close season, Tottenham were due to travel on a much-needed money-spinning tour to Japan. A trip of this nature required a lot of organisation and planning so a few weeks before the team were due to fly out, Terry Venables said to me, 'John, I want you to stay here to look after Gazza and treat the other injured players. Dave Butler will come to Japan and look after the lads while we are away.' To say I was relieved was an understatement, as after years of travelling around the world I was definitely happier staying at home. Paul was still one of the club's star players and even though he was injured the Japanese organisers wanted him to go. When Terry discovered this, he came to see me and asked if I would like to go on the trip with Paul. No chance I thought, so I politely declined. The rehab was still in the initial stage so there was no chance I would allow him to be stuck on a plane for such a considerable amount of time, and he would also be forced to make numerous guest appearances. The best thing for his rehabilitation was to stay in London and continue working hard alongside the other injured lads. I'm sure Terry wasn't too happy about my decision, but the players' welfare and best interests always have to come first.

In modern-day football the medical team of Premier League and Championship clubs can be made up of a large number of staff, including a club doctor, head physiotherapist, senior physiotherapist, physiotherapist, masseurs, fitness and conditioning coach, sports scientists, strength and power coach – and this is just for the first team. The academy players also enjoy their own designated medical staff as well. But back in the late 1980s and early '90s it was a completely different story. Tottenham's medical staff consisted of Dr Brian Curtin, myself, my assistant Dave Butler and a couple of part-time physios to cover the youth matches on a Saturday morning. The day-to-day running of the treatment room normally consisted of myself treating the players and also planning and monitoring the rehab of the long-term injuries. Dave's role was to help prepare the players for training and then continue with the rehab out on the field, at which he excelled. Due to the sheer number of professionals and apprentices under our care, it quickly became apparent that I somehow had to find more time to focus on Paul.

My only option was to get into work earlier, which meant getting up at 6am and after a quick slice of toast and cup of tea I would join the early-morning commuters on the M1 and head to London. Paul would meet me at the training ground at 8am and we would immediately get to work. This new schedule worked really well as it allowed us to carry out valuable one-to-one rehab before the other players arrived. I would then send him for a coffee break mid-morning while myself and Dave prepared the players for training and I could start the other injured players on their individual rehab programmes.

However, one particular morning sticks in my mind. After our normal early-morning session, it was time for Paul to have a break and go for a drink but because some of the other lads were enjoying a bit of banter, he decided to stick around in the treatment room. Paul being Paul, he was the centre of attention and fooling around, being a real pain in the arse, so I abruptly told him, 'Piss off out of the treatment room.' He looked shocked and upset as I rarely lost my temper. It had the desired effect because he stormed towards the door and slammed it as he left. About half an hour later there was a knock at the door. I opened it and to my astonishment Paul was standing there with a white rose in his mouth. 'Sorry,' he said and held out his hand. 'Are we still mates?' Trying not to laugh, I said, 'Of course we are and always will be as long as you behave yourself.' That was the only cross word we had during that year. There was a mutual respect between us; he knew I was going to do everything in my power to get him back playing at the highest level and I knew he had the drive to come back stronger, fitter and better than before.

Paul came in one morning for his usual early session and said, 'John, how do you feel about a working holiday to Portugal?' He then went on to explain that he had been speaking to one of the tabloid papers and they were prepared to fund the trip in return for a few exclusive photos. It was a tempting offer and after the emotion of the past few weeks, I thought it would be a good opportunity for us both to recharge our batteries while still working hard. After consulting with the club and surgeon, it was agreed we would fly to Portugal for a ten-day break and continue with our strict rehab programme.

The day of the trip arrived but as soon as we reached the airport, I realised it wasn't just going to be myself and Paul. In actual fact there was a large party of us flying out to enjoy the sunny surroundings of Portugal. The group consisted of myself, Paul, his dad John who was good company for me, his ball-juggling brother-in-law also called John, his sidekick Jimmy 'Five Bellies' Gardner and his friend Terry Bailey, who was then married to Linda Lusardi. To complete the group was the Chrysalis Films crew, who had been given permission to document Paul's rehab from start to finish. They were led by Neil Duncanson and Ken McNeil. Both Neil and Ken became good friends during this period of my life. They were always respectful when on duty and after a while I forgot that the cameras were there. As our group walked through the airport we were met by loud cheers from the public as they spotted Gazza. I'm sure the Crazy Gang had nothing on our motley crew!

By the time we arrived at our beautiful hotel on the harbour of Vilamoura it was late afternoon. After going our separate ways to unpack we agreed to meet that evening for a drink and unwind after a long day of travelling. I decided to leave my room a few minutes early to explore the facilities the hotel had and what we could use for the following morning's session. As I opened the door to the pool area, I was met by the sight of a tall blonde lady I instantly recognised as the famous Danish actress Brigitte Nielsen, who was then married to Sylvester Stallone. I then realised that the decision to head there instead of continuing the rehabilitation in the Portakabins of a rainy Mill Hill was a good one.

This trip laid the foundation for Paul's rehab. The atmosphere was brilliant within the group and we worked extremely hard throughout our morning and afternoon sessions. Due to the excellent progress he had made, these sessions now included a full range of muscle and joint exercises. I was also able to add a small amount of resistance, which was achieved with the help of a couple of diving belts that I managed to purchase early one morning on the quayside. These weights were a godsend and were used throughout his rehab, and they especially came into their own during his hydrotherapy sessions in the pool. We were achieving so much in the sunny surroundings of the hotel; he was working extremely hard and I had to make sure he didn't push himself too much and jeopardise all our good work. In between our sessions we enjoyed a lot of fun and laughter. One of the highlights was a game of table tennis with Brigitte. That table got a lot of use throughout our break but even though he was on crutches and one leg Paul was too good for us all.

A few days into our trip we were enjoying an evening meal when all of a sudden Gazza said to us all, 'Who fancies an afternoon of shark fishing? I have arranged a boat; the skipper will take us about 14 miles out to sea where it will be teeming with sharks!' A few of the lads didn't seem too overjoyed with the proposition but as Paul is such an avid fisherman and his progress was excellent, I thought it would be a great idea. We arrived the next morning on the quayside to be met by the sight of a small white boat, and suddenly there were a few anxious faces as it didn't seem big enough to take on the vast expanse of shark-infested waters. Jimmy seemed especially worried and it wouldn't have surprised me if Paul was going to make him walk the plank.

As we left dry land and stepped on board, Paul said to me, 'John, why don't you go up in the crow's nest? You will get a great view of the luxury yachts and lovely scenery.' This sounded a great idea, so somehow I scrambled my way up the mast and made myself comfy. As we set sail, I felt relaxed looking at the lovely clear blue water as the Mediterranean sun shone down. Unfortunately this didn't last long; as we navigated into the open sea it started to get windy and the waves started crashing into our boat, making it rock from side to side. I decided to try and get down to the relative safety of the deck and as I attempted to do so the boat hit an almighty wave, forcing me to hang on for dear life with my feet inches from the water. Paul was laughing and shouted, 'John, you will have to stay up there until it is a bit calmer.' I decided this was maybe the best bit of advice he had ever given me. As I looked down from my lofty position, I realised it wasn't just me in a spot of trouble as John and Jimmy were scrambling around on all fours trying not to bring up their breakfast. Eventually the sea became a bit calmer and Paul threw me a can of beer to enjoy before we came to a stop to start fishing. When I finally managed to get my feet back on deck there were still a couple of the lads looking a bit worse for wear. The mood soon changed as the fishing rods came out, but I did feel sorry for the camera crew as while we were fishing for sharks, they were in a rubber dinghy that was tied to our boat about 100 yards away!

Paul was in his element. I sometimes felt that despite all the hype and razzmatazz that followed him, he was only truly happy when he was away from it all and fishing by himself. Most of us

129

had a turn but with varying degrees of success; we managed to catch a few fish but there was still no sign of the elusive shark. Finally one of the rods showed a large bite. Whatever was on the end of the line it wasn't giving up without a fight, and after an almighty battle Paul managed to bring the catch close to our boat. As we cautiously peered over the edge, it was pleasing to see a baby shark in the water. The skipper carefully brought it on to deck and Paul said, 'Give it to Johnny.' Thanks Gazza, I thought, as I was handed the shark. The skipper said to me, 'Whatever you do, don't drop it as it will bite somebody's leg off.' Imagine the headlines: 'Paul Gascoigne gets his good leg bitten off by his physio'! After holding the shark for a short while and chasing Gazza with it I put the thrashing beast over the side and back into the sea where it belonged, and not on the barbecue it was destined for.

We returned from Portugal not only with a nice tan but also refreshed and ready for the next stage of rehabilitation. It had been an intense ten days and we had both worked very hard. The varied exercise protocol was paying dividends and by the time we visited John Browett on 10 July, Paul's knee displayed minimal swelling and increased movement from 0 to 95 degrees. John was delighted and advised us that it was safe to wean Paul off the brace and only use it when he was in an outdoor environment.

The good news we received from John unfortunately highlighted a big problem in the next stage of rehabilitation. I realised that for Paul to take the next step in his fightback, two Portakabins stuck in the corner of a car park wouldn't be sufficient and somehow I needed to find better facilities.

Help came from a lovely man called John Coberman, who used to spend a lot of time at the training ground where he would drive players around and run errands for them. As soon as he learned of my frustration with the facilities, he mentioned that he was a member of the Dolphin Leisure Club in Mill Hill, which had a fantastic pool and gym. I asked if he could arrange a meeting for me with the manager, so John kindly went away and set up an appointment to see him. A few days later I travelled there to try and negotiate a deal. The manager was brilliant and kindly agreed to give me free passes for our injured players. This was a godsend as it gave us access to their well-equipped gym but more importantly a swimming pool. The use of a pool allowed me to plan and conduct hydrotherapy sessions. Erik Thorstvedt mentioned that in Norway a common rehabilitation technique was deep-water running, so after much research I purchased four buoyancy vests, which kept the players upright and non-weight bearing while running in water. The daily visits there enabled Paul to swim, deep-water run and have full use of their gym. It took me a lot of time to devise daily programmes for him and he often said, 'John, you have more programmes than Radio 2!'

Due to the excellent progress we had made, it was decided to remove the wires from Paul's knee. They gave stability to the patella but had started to become an irritation and were holding up further progression in his rehabilitation. This procedure was carried out under general anaesthetic by John on 4 September 1991. For a short while we had to plateau Paul's rehab to allow the wound to heal but all indications showed his knee had regained full stability.

Part of the transfer agreement between Spurs and Lazio was for Paul to make an occasional trip to Rome. These allowed the fanatical Lazio supporters to see him and also the medical staff to check on his progress. On the first visit it was agreed for Paul's close friend Glenn Roeder to accompany him. Glenn had a distinguished playing career as a central defender for teams such as Queens Park Rangers, Newcastle United and Watford, and also went on to manage in the Premier League with West Ham United, Newcastle United and Norwich City. I believe it was when Glenn was a player at Newcastle in the mid-1980s that he first formed a close bond with Paul, so he was the perfect person to accompany him to Rome as he was older and a calming influence. When they returned, Paul told me that the trip was a success, the Lazio fans adored him and he couldn't wait to return and play in front of them. He has always been driven and hard-working but I believe this trip gave him an extra spark to get back to full fitness.

Shortly after Paul had suffered his initial injury, another high-profile London footballer suffered a similar ruptured anterior cruciate ligament. The rehabilitation protocols for this player were completely different to ours; he had flown out to the United States for a pioneering operation which involved an achilles tendon of a deceased man being implanted to replace his own ruptured tendon. A national tabloid decided to compare the progress of both players to see which method of rehabilitation was the best, which was extremely unfair as no two injuries are the same. Both of the players' fitness battles were being played out in the public eye, which certainly increased the pressure, while I also had the film crew following us around and videoing our every move.

For several months the other player's surgery seemed to be a success, but unfortunately the donor tendon had stretched and was no longer performing as it should. The result of this setback meant more major surgery, this time using a replacement tendon from his own leg and meant a further ten months out of football, but I was delighted to see him return to full fitness and have many more years in the game.

Despite the skill and expert knowledge of all the surgeons I have had the pleasure to watch, I would sometimes get some crude advice in regards to Paul's recovery. I lost count of the number of letters and phone calls from manufacturers asking me to use their products to aid his return to fitness. Terry Venables always asked me to either write or call them back to help maintain good public relations for the club. There is one particular letter that will always stick in my mind, which read:

Dear Mr Sheridan

I have been following your progress with Paul Gascoigne and have a product which will help shorten his recovery. Please ring me on my number 01*** ****48.

Yours sincerely,

Fred Bloggs

Hawthorn Farm

The following day I phoned the farmer and introduced myself. The farmer said, 'It's a natural remedy that will definitely help him.' Intrigued, I asked him to share his secret, and he said, 'It is good old-fashioned cow manure with added medicinal herbs. You need to warm it up and spread it over his knee to make a hot poultice, it stinks a bit but if you can stand the smell it will speed up the healing process.' I was shocked and had visions of one of the best players in the world laying on the treatment table with a lump of cow shit on his knee, then Terry walking in saying, 'What is that smell?'

The farmer meant well so I decided to let him down gently. 'What breed of cows have you got?' I asked. 'Guernsey,' he replied. 'That's a shame, because Paul is a northerner, we are only allowed to use Aberdeen Angus I'm afraid but thank you very much for your help.' I had a little chuckle as I put down the phone. A few days later Terry asked if I had called the farmer so I replied, 'I did, Terry, but unfortunately it was a load of old crap!'

11

Disaster and the Fightback Begins Again

BY THE time myself and Paul went to see John Browett for a check-up on 21 September 1991 we were both feeling extremely positive. This was well founded when the surgeon confirmed that the knee had settled extremely well and he was delighted with the progress we had made so far.

A week later, Paul went back to his home city of Newcastle to visit his family. In the early hours of Saturday, 29 September, I received a phone call from the Royal Victoria Infirmary in Newcastle informing me they had admitted Paul after he had been assaulted in a nightclub. I was told he had sustained bruising to his face, a chipped tooth and minimal damage to the medial collateral ligament in his right knee. A distraught Gazza took the phone and said, 'John, they have got it wrong, I know it is worse than they are saying.' I told him to let me speak to the doctor and was put on to a tired-sounding female who said, 'Hello John, this is the duty doctor. I have examined his right knee and there seems to be minor damage to his medial ligament.' I replied, 'Paul seems to think it is a lot worse.' She said, 'He has had a thorough examination and that is the only injury I have found.' Paul came back on the phone and said, 'I am leaving the hospital and coming to see you. Jimmy will drive me down now.'

I told Paul to meet me at the training ground, so after travelling through the night he hobbled into the treatment room on a wet Sunday morning still in his hospital gown and in a lot of pain. It was obvious to see that there was more to this than minor ligament damage. I remained calm as I started to examine Paul's knee but immediately my heart sank as I realised the patella was missing and instead where it should have been was just a huge gap. Further examination showed he had sustained a transverse fracture of the right patella with associate damage to the retinacular ligamentous structure on both sides of the knee. This was another career-threatening injury; the only blessing was that the anterior cruciate ligament graft was still intact.

I immediately arranged for a mobile x-ray unit to come to the training ground and phoned John to explain what had happened over the past few hours. John was great and said, 'I will be there as soon as possible.' He was true to his word and within an hour had arrived and examined Paul; he agreed with my diagnosis and unfortunately this confirmed our worst fears – the x-ray showed the fracture was extremely nasty and required immediate surgery. John made arrangements at Princess Grace Hospital and that evening he carried out the operation. Once again he performed a minor miracle by bringing the fractured parts of the patella together and lined up the articular surface with an image intensifier. To keep the patella in place he used tension band wiring.

The operation was deemed a success but Paul's career was again in doubt. Lazio and their medical team were informed, and Dr Claudio Bartolina flew over from the Italian club to see myself and visit Paul in hospital. After examining the scans and x-rays he made the following statement to the press, 'The new injury is very serious. I don't think he will pass our medical tests on his knee. It is difficult to see how he will be ready for a medical test on 30 May [1992]. He must be fit to play a full match by then or the contract fails.' Ever since Paul had suffered his initial injury in the FA Cup Final, I had felt under pressure to get him back to full fitness but with this second injury and Dr Bartolina's statement the pressure was ramped up to an almost unbearable level.

One of the questions that was being asked by both clubs and the surgeon was why the fracture was missed at the hospital in Newcastle. I had also wondered why such an obvious injury was overlooked, but I had visions of an overworked junior doctor worried sick that her career could be in tatters. A few days later the phone rang in the treatment room. It was the doctor from Newcastle and she asked how Paul was. I explained what had happened in the period between that call and him having left the hospital after the assault. She seemed horrified and asked me, 'What are you going to do about it?' I replied, 'If the club decide to pursue it then it will be difficult for me to stop them, but to my mind I'm sure you have learned from it and will never miss the injury again and I don't want to jeopardise your career.' To the best of my knowledge the doctor wasn't investigated by either club and I am sure that she went on to have a successful, rewarding and hard-working career within the NHS.

After just over a week in hospital, Paul was discharged on 9 October with the injured knee in a brace. While recuperating at home for the next eight weeks he used a continuous passive motion machine which gently mobilised the joint, and nearer the end of this period he was allowed to visit me at my practice in Luton so we could concentrate in complete privacy on getting him fit to play at the highest level again. The knee continued to react well to the treatment and this was definitely helped by all the hard work we had undertaken prior to this second injury. In mid-November I organised for the knee to be x-rayed, which showed the fracture was healing well and Mr Browett allowed Paul to fully bear weight while in a brace. We were now able to step up his rehabilitation programme and by the middle of December the fracture line was obliterating. After everything that had happened, I truly believed we must have had a guardian angel looking after us.

Even though we were seemingly back on track with the long road to fitness, I believe the constant pressure was starting to take its toll on me. I often felt completely on my own, I lacked support from the club and it appeared that certain people were waiting for us to fail. Looking back, I believe we used this as a positive to keep driving on and it made us more determined to prove all the doubters wrong. During this period, the left hip that I had damaged in childhood was starting to give me a lot of pain so I had it x-rayed at the club. This showed that the ball and socket joint had deteriorated badly and was in danger of collapsing. This was the last thing I needed so I had a little prayer asking for it not to get any worse until after Paul's medical with Lazio, then I could think about myself and explore the possibility of a hip replacement.

By mid-January Paul was able to jog comfortably without the leg brace, then further x-rays and a tomogram scan showed that the patella had healed well and even though we had a few setbacks along the way the rehabilitation was going from strength to strength. The doubters were maybe looking on now with a bit more optimism. Throughout February, Paul constantly worked hard every day at the training ground but still continued to make the occasional trip to my practice in Luton to undertake extra rehab away from all prying eyes. However, I did start to notice the odd press photographer parked outside my house looking for any opportunity to get a snap.

March came and after further tests it was decided that the patella had healed soundly and the supporting wires were now able to be removed. This was a real boost as if we had any chance of being ready to pass the stringent medical then it had to be done at this point in time. So under a general anaesthetic the wires were removed. We then checked his knee using an MRI scan and the results showed no untoward issues following the operation. After a short plateau in Paul's rehab, which allowed small stresses to gradually go through the patella, his programme was increased to allow more intense running, twisting, turning, swimming and gym work. The field work was overseen by my assistant Dave Butler who excelled when working with Paul out on the grass.

After a visit to Harley Street to see John Browett in the middle of April, a big milestone was reached. Paul was now allowed to join in with controlled small-sided games, and I am sure this was the point that the Lazio officials believed there was a chance they were going to get their player. To be fair to Lazio, they had been very good and supportive during the rehabilitation process. I had built up a good relationship with both the football and medical officials and they often complimented our rehabilitation programmes and protocols.

The fitness test to determine if all of our hard work over the past 12 months had been successful started on 18 May 1992, a year to the day since Paul's first operation. This date is unforgettable for me as it is my wedding anniversary but I was hoping for a better day than the previous year. The Lazio officials, in conjunction with the highly acclaimed orthopaedic surgeon Jim Andrews, had devised the most stringent medical I have ever experienced. This surgeon was recognised as the world's leading expert on knees and would have the final decision as to whether the transfer would go ahead. The tests would be in two parts; the first four days would be held at our training ground in Mill Hill and would be overseen by Lazio's club doctor Claudio Bartolini, then the second part would be held in Italy for two days. Mr Andrews would be in attendance and we would finally learn our fate.

The six days of the medical would be hell for both myself and Paul, physically for him and mentally for me. The first part consisted of a full analytical check of the injured knee and leg, a full Cybex test to check the mobility and strength of the knee, followed by running, turning, jumping, hopping, kicking everything but the kitchen sink. The Cybex test used an Akron isokinetic therapy machine, which even then cost £22,000 to buy, and would be programmed to a player's personal requirements with the computer then updating the exercises as his condition improves.

Day four would include a 60-minute 11v11 match between Tottenham's first team and reserves. Despite everything that was at stake, Paul appeared positive and ready for all the trials and tribulations that he was about to undertake. Throughout the four days he did everything that was asked of him and his knee showed no negative reactions to the physical exertions he was put through. In fact, he finished day four on a physical and mental high as he ran riot in the match against the reserves, scoring all four goals in a 4-2 victory which he celebrated by diving head-first in a puddle of water watched by his beloved dad. The Lazio officials headed back to Rome seemingly pleased with the progress so far, saying, 'Paul moved quite smoothly and showed no psychological issues from his four operations. The evidence is promising but we will take time to evaluate the findings so far.' They thanked both myself and Dave Butler for the way the first part of the fitness test was conducted and as they left, I breathed a huge sigh of relief and looked forward to a good night's sleep.

On Friday, 22 May, myself and Paul flew to Rome to complete the final part of the fitness test. As we entered the airport we were greeted with mass hysteria from the fanatical Lazio supporters, which was something I had never seen anything like before. The large crowd were singing Paul's name and trying to touch him, while the security guards were struggling not to get overrun by the boisterous and passionate fans. This was the complete opposite from his visit to Rome in August when he was half-crippled on crutches surrounded by friends, bodyguards, hangers-on and a small posse of supporters. This time he was accompanied by a tight-knit group of people who had his best interests at heart and were desperate for him to finally complete the life-changing transfer. Paul looked like and conducted himself as a mature young man who was determined to resurrect his bright career. With the footballing world now holding its breath, would he pass or fail at the final stage?

The last part of the fitness test was due to start on Monday, 25 May and would be held at both the Olympic Stadium and the Lazio training ground. However, unbeknown to us, Jim Andrews had flown in earlier than expected, and he called and asked if he could examine Paul's knee before the planned medical. So I had to make a clear and concise decision that would be in the best interests of the club, player and my conscience. This was my reputation on the line and I knew for sure that if he failed to meet Lazio's extremely high standards

141

then it would be my head on the chopping block and it wouldn't just be Paul's career on the scrapheap.

I didn't have anything to hide so I happily agreed and we went to meet Mr Andrews that night. The club sent a car to pick us up and drove us to a clinic in Rome, where we were greeted by a small group of Lazio officials and the highly acclaimed surgeon. After exchanging pleasantries, he asked me if I had the medical records of the entire rehabilitation process. Once again, my daughter Debbie had come up trumps as she had prepared a folder with all the information he required. Dr Andrews was at the top of his occupation and his patients included the great Jack Nicklaus and the superstar basketball player Michael Jordan. It was obvious he wouldn't suffer fools gladly and proceeded with the fitness test with 100 per cent professionalism. He examined Paul with hardly a word spoken, and finally he said, 'Okay, Paul, I will see you on Monday after I have studied the videos from Mill Hill and read your physiotherapist's medical records. Thank you for seeing me early Mr Sheridan and for having all the data at hand. You are very professional in your approach.' With that he shook our hands and we left the clinic none the wiser. 'How did that go, John?' said Paul. 'I'm not sure, but he knows we are not concealing anything and without doubt it was the correct thing to do to let him examine you. It's Sunday tomorrow and I think you should get as much rest as you can because on Monday, they are going to run you ragged.'

We returned to the hotel and I went to bed knowing I had made the right decision. Even though the Lazio officials and medical team had made me feel most welcome I still felt quite isolated and upset that I was shouldering the burden of this multi-million-pound transfer, because Terry Venables, John

Browett and the club's legal team were due to fly out in the next few days but until then it was down to me.

On Sunday evening we decided to go out for an al fresco meal at one of Rome's famous restaurants. We had just finished our main course when along came Lazio's officials and medical staff, accompanied by Jim Andrews. After they had taken their seats, I quietly said to Paul, 'After our dessert we will leave quietly and head back to the hotel for an early night.' He wanted to stay and have a couple of drinks to relax and said, 'John, they know what I am like. I can't change who I am.' I replied, 'Paul, nobody wants you to change but if we get up and leave quietly, we will create a great impression before tomorrow's fitness test.' So after finishing our meal we got up and left, and while passing the Lazio table we said, 'Goodnight, see you in the morning.' I overhead Jim Andrews say quietly to the club doctor, 'What a fine young athlete,' and he then said to us, 'Have a good sleep and see you tomorrow.' I think an early night suited us all as we felt drained after a hectic and emotional couple of days.

Monday morning came and we got up in a positive mood but nervous for what the day might bring. A car from Lazio arrived at the hotel to transport our group to the training ground. As soon we arrived it became apparent that the eyes of the world would be watching us as there were TV cameras and media lining the road to the entrance to the ground. The Lazio staff and officials were most welcoming but there was an underlying feeling of anticipation to see if Paul had fully recovered. To his credit, Gazza showed no signs of nervousness and pulled out all the stops throughout an extremely hard physical session which would have had a lesser person on their knees. After more stringent tests by Jim Andrews and the Lazio medical staff, we were still no closer to finding out the verdict as the day drew to a close. Myself and Paul headed back to the hotel knowing we couldn't have done any more. The press conference was due to be held later on that evening when not just us but also the world would discover if Gazza had become a Lazio player.

As we entered the hotel the overriding feeling was of exhaustion. Paul went straight up to bed to get some rest and I headed for the bar to try and relax. When looking back at photos of me from that time, I can clearly see I look on the verge of a breakdown. Sitting alone at the bar, I quietly contemplated and reflected on the last few days and months. My thoughts turned to my family and I just wanted to get home to see them. A few moments later, I heard a voice say, 'John, can I join you?' I looked round and recognised a *Daily Mirror* reporter who had travelled out to Rome to cover the story. He said, 'Have you heard the result of the fitness test?' I replied, 'No, not yet.' He said, 'Well done, you did it. Paul has passed with flying colours.' Suddenly the enormity of what had happened over the past 12 months hit me and I slumped forward on to the bar with tears rolling down my cheeks. I felt physically and mentally drained; all the doubters who said he would never play again at the highest level had been proved wrong. I could return home with my head held high and Paul could look forward to enjoying his Italian adventure.

Lazio released a statement confirming the transfer, 'All doubts have been removed about Paul Gascoigne's fitness. This has been reinforced by Mr Jim Andrews who had been invited to Rome by Lazio at huge expense to pass the final verdict after all the data had been collated. He remarked Paul is as good as ever and his recovery and recuperation in London has been remarkable. The Tottenham physiotherapist John Sheridan deserves a lot of praise. It was a supreme effort by him and the rest of the medical team.'

So on Monday, 25 May, five days before the initial deadline, Paul was finally passed fit. My last remedial programme was given to the club before he embarked on his move to Lazio. This had been carefully planned so he could progress smoothly into full training in Italy. I was confident he was going to be in good hands as I respected and trusted the medical team at Lazio.

Just before travelling back to England, a senior Lazio official approached me and asked if I would consider moving to Italy to join them and also go on their pre-season tour to Canada and Brazil. I felt that over the past 12 months I had been taken for granted by Tottenham and as I hadn't signed a contract with the club it was a very tempting offer. However, I was extremely tired and the thought of travelling all over the world at my age and uprooting my family with a move to Italy was not one that appealed to me. In fact, after everything that had happened over the past year, I just wanted to spend more time at home. The recent events had taken their toll on my health, especially my left hip which continued to give me bouts of pain. I therefore told Lazio that I was extremely flattered by their offer and if I was a few years younger I would have loved to join them but regrettably the answer was no. However, if they ever needed my support or advice, I would always be prepared to help them.

Upon returning to England I received a lot of nice letters and compliments from the medical establishment. One was from the Cambridgeshire surgeon Bernard Meggitt, who I respected and had got to know since my days at Luton. He wrote, 'Success for you and physiotherapy nationally.' A couple of years later the Chartered Society of Physiotherapy asked if they could feature Paul's rehabilitation in their centenary exhibition in 1994. I felt this was an honour of the highest nature, which left me feeling extremely proud of the achievement.

The film crew who had followed our every move released their programme, *Gazza: The Fightback*. It was aired for prime time viewing and showed the highs, lows and emotion of the journey to get Paul back to full fitness. It received fantastic reviews and these days I occasionally sit down to watch it and relive that crazy year in my life.

A few months after the medical, I returned to Rome for one last time after being invited by Paul and the club to see how he had settled. I was made to feel most welcome by the Lazio medical staff and it turned into a busman's holiday as I was given a club tracksuit and asked to treat some of the club's star players. While staying with Paul in his villa, I soon realised he was worshipped by the people of Rome. He took me sightseeing to the magnificent Colosseum and then we walked down the Spanish steps to the Trevi Fountain. As I threw a coin into the water, I made a wish that he would enjoy a long and successful career. Everywhere we went Paul was mobbed by fans. I felt sorry for him that he was unable to enjoy any privacy.

I will always remember my few visits to Rome, especially the magnificent sights but more importantly the friendliness shown to me by the Italian people and club officials. That was the last time I saw Paul in person as he got on with his career and life in Italy and I returned to mine in England. However, I did speak to him again but in unfortunate circumstances. In April 1994 I received a phone call and heard Paul's distraught voice. He was on a stretcher after just sustaining a broken leg while tackling team-mate Alessandro Nesta in training and wanted some reassurance that he would be okay. Again, he was worldwide news and somehow the media found out about the call, so it wasn't long before I was besieged by the national press asking me to spill the beans on Paul. I politely declined and kept a respectable silence.

I have read on numerous occasions that some people think he was never the same player after his knee injury. I disagree and I think his achievements after returning to full fitness speak for themselves.

Before the injury

	Appearances	Goals
Club	184	40
International	20	2

After the injury

	Appearances	Goals
Club	204	47
International	37	8

By the 1995/96 season Paul had been transferred to Glasgow Rangers where he won both the PFA Scotland Players' Player of the Year and the SFWA Footballer of the Year awards. He was also selected in the UEFA European Championship team of the tournament in 1996 and is scorer of arguably the greatest England goal of all time with the famous volley against Scotland at Wembley in that summer's finals. I think you can agree that if he wasn't back to his best, he wouldn't have been able to continue playing at this level for such a sustained period of time.

Chapter 12

The Beginning of the
End at Tottenham

I RETURNED home from Italy emotional and exhausted. After enjoying some quality time with my family during the summer of 1992, the thought of going back to the daily grind of professional football filled me with dread. Deep down I knew I had lost my spark for football and was not looking forward to the coming season. Throughout my career I have always given 100 per cent, but I questioned if, after everything that had happened throughout the last 12 months, I would still be able to do so. I confided in my trusted friend Dr Brian Curtin and explained that I was considering leaving. He understood but asked me to stay on for one more year as he was planning to retire at the end of the season and we could leave together. We had grown close over the past few years, so after a little bit of persuasion I agreed to stay. I didn't mention it to anybody else and set about getting ready for pre-season.

The performances on the pitch over the past year had been disappointing and due to this lack of form it was upsetting when manager Peter Shreeves paid the price with the loss of his job. However, his replacements for the coming season were Doug Livermore and Ray Clemence, who were both stepping up from coaching positions to become joint managers of the first team. I enjoyed great relationships with Doug and Ray and this made my decision to stay on for a further year a little bit easier. The upcoming season was the first year of the Premier League and Spurs had made some great signings over the summer, including centre-forward Teddy Sheringham for a then club record £2.1m and also the highly rated young winger Darren Anderton from Portsmouth. This meant the players, staff and supporters approached the season with renewed optimism.

Over the next few months my hip continued to deteriorate and I was in constant discomfort so in October I went to see the highly renowned hip surgeon Richard Villar in Cambridge. After an initial examination and further tests, he told me I was in desperate need of a replacement and agreed to carry out the operation the following month. Unfortunately he couldn't guarantee the success of the replacement hip due to the extensive damage I suffered as a child and the subsequent deterioration. However, Mr Villar was a man who gave me immense confidence and I felt extremely privileged to have a world-class surgeon operate on me. I later learned that he was an ex-SAS surgeon and also a member of a group called Medical Emergency Relief International (Merlin). He was a very brave man and as a member of Merlin often found himself at the forefront of major catastrophes all around the world.

After the appointment I returned to the club and explained to Terry Venables that the surgeon had recommended a hip replacement. To his credit, Terry kindly allowed me to take some time off during the season to undergo the operation. I'm sure he could see the amount of pain I was in and I would like to think it was a small reward and appreciation for helping to get Paul Gascoigne fit. So on 24 November 1992 I reported to the BUPA hospital in preparation for the procedure the following day. After a five-hour operation I remember waking up with no pain and the constant discomfort in my hip was gone. A few days later, Gary Mabbutt and Nayim made the long journey to visit me in hospital. These were two of my favourite players and I enjoyed a close relationship with them both.

My rehab started in earnest with their very competent physiotherapy team. I didn't need any motivation as I had been given a second chance and was going to grab it with both hands. My stay in hospital was due to last for two weeks, and during the second week I was asked by one of the physios if I could help with one of their patients. They said he had also had a hip replacement but was scared to get out of bed. One of the staff discovered he was a Tottenham fan and thought it might be a good idea if I could speak to him and encourage him to get up and about. He was soon out of his bed after I promised to get him the Spurs players' autographs and I even challenged him to a race on our crutches along the corridor! Twenty-eight years later my hip replacement is still going strong and even though I'm a lot older now, I can still play a regular game of golf and swim on almost a daily basis. I honestly cannot thank Mr Villar enough for the quality of life his skill and expertise has allowed me to enjoy.

After a few weeks recuperating at home I thought it would be a good idea to go away for a short break to help recharge my batteries for the next step of rehabilitation, so I booked a week's holiday in Malta with my wife and daughter who had both cared for me during my recovery. Unbeknown to the three of us, the Malta branch of the Tottenham supporters' club had somehow discovered I was visiting. After landing at Valletta airport I struggled off the plane with my two crutches, tired and in a lot of discomfort. To my amazement I was greeted by a welcoming party and discovered they had kindly planned an extensive programme of sightseeing, meals and excursions throughout the duration of our stay. This was the last thing I needed as all I wanted to do was enjoy a week of rest and relaxation, so in my haste I was rude to the chairman of the supporters' club and told him how I felt. Looking back, I not only embarrassed myself but also Betty and Debbie. After arriving at the hotel, I calmed down and realised my conduct at the airport was unacceptable. So I immediately contacted the supporters' club committee to apologise and invite them to our hotel the following day to have lunch. I explained to them what I had been through during the last few months and to help repair any damage I agreed to a shortened programme of sightseeing which culminated in a Q&A session at their clubhouse near the end of our stay. The supporters' club was made up of some of the local dignitaries and I discovered one of them had kindly arranged for an upgrade at our hotel to the penthouse suite.

Myself, Betty and Debbie had a lovely week and made some good friends; their hospitality was second to none and we especially enjoyed the tour of the island in a police car. For a long time, I kept in touch with many of these lovely people and they continued to send me their official journal every year. Whenever any of the supporters' club travelled over from Malta for a Tottenham game, I would always invite them to my home in Luton for a meal. I often look back at my conduct at the airport and would like to think it was the trauma of the operation and the stress of getting Gazza fit that made me act in a very uncharacteristic fashion. Definitely it was a lesson learned.

After recuperating at home for a couple more months I returned to Tottenham in late February with a renewed zest for the remainder of the season. I was pleased to find that Dave Butler had coped well in my absence, the players were happy to see me back and I was delighted to be treating them again. To allow me to return to work I had to badger the surgeon, who reluctantly agreed on the proviso that I would continue to use a walking stick, work on alternate days and also only attend home matches. He also asked me to remember that I had undergone a major operation and it would take some time to return to full strength, but I was relieved to get back to some sort of normality. Ray and Doug had done well with the team and were enjoying a good season, culminating in an FA Cup semi-final appearance and a respectable position in the league. However, it soon became apparent that I had retuned too early. I was feeling extremely tired as the workload and commuting became too much; this confirmed that the decision to leave at the end of the season was the correct one.

I continued to give 100 per cent and wanted to leave the medical department in a good position, but every time I asked for a new piece of medical equipment my request was turned down due to lack of funds. This became frustrating as for the last few years it felt as if we were doing our job with one hand tied behind our backs. The constant frustration and lack of support came to a head in early spring. I was getting the players ready for training when I received a phone call from Terry Venables informing me that he had called a meeting at lunchtime and I had to attend. A short while later, Dave Butler walked into the treatment room. I said, 'Dave, do you know what this meeting is about?' He replied, 'It is about Vinny Samways missing training yesterday.' Vinny had a slight knock and was due in for treatment with Dave but didn't come in as he was stuck in traffic, so instead he went to train at a local park. As it was one of my days off, I wasn't aware of what had happened until I came in that day. Vinny told me that he had tried to call but couldn't get through and I was more than happy with his explanation. I treated him and he was fit to train with the rest of the players, but I couldn't believe Dave had mentioned it to Terry because as far as I was concerned the matter was closed.

Lunchtime came and I went to Terry's office for the meeting alongside Ray, Doug and Dave. As chief executive, Terry had a lot of pressure on his shoulders and I sensed he wasn't in one of his better moods. 'What happened to Vinny Samways yesterday?' he said gruffly. I replied, 'I don't know, Terry, ask Dave.' 'Where were you, why weren't you in?' Terry said. I couldn't believe it. After what had gone on over the past 18 months and despite undergoing a major operation, it showed that he expected me to function in a normal manner even though I wasn't in a fit state to return to my usual workload.

I bluntly told him, 'If you don't know by now Terry then I am not going to tell you.' He replied, 'You know your problem John, you are too soft with the players. From now on you need to be a lot harder with them.' I was fuming so replied, 'Terry, what you see is what you get and I am not going to change after all these years.' Suddenly the blame for Vinny not training was being shifted towards me. Something snapped inside and I realised enough was enough, but I was extremely disappointed and too tired to argue anymore. To stop Vinny getting fined I agreed that if he came to my house that evening for treatment, he would get away without losing any money. As I walked out of the office, I knew that it was the end of the road for me at the club.

The players' grapevine had been busy and a short while later Vinny came to see me and said, 'Sorry John.' I replied,

'Don't worry Vinny, it's not your fault. As long as you come to my house tonight you won't get fined.' He was as good as gold and turned up at my home in Luton on time. I checked the injury to make sure he was still okay and afterwards we had a cup of tea and had a chat about the events of the day. However, unbeknown to Vinny, I had already asked my daughter Debbie to type my resignation letter. To their credit Ray and Doug called me that evening as they must have sensed what I was going to do. I appreciated their calls and despite their best efforts to change my mind I knew the end of my time at Tottenham was quickly approaching. It was not the way I wanted to leave the club but in my heart of hearts I knew it was the right decision. I had always given 100 per cent, often to the detriment of my family and health, and it showed that certain people didn't really care about my mental and physical health.

The next morning, I drove to the training ground and immediately went to see Terry in his office. As I went in, I handed him my resignation letter. He immediately opened it and asked why I had come to the decision. I replied, 'I don't enjoy it anymore, Terry, and I don't feel I can carry out my job with the enthusiasm I once could. I will stay on until a replacement can be found as I don't want to let down the players who are still undergoing rehab.' As I left his office, I knew it was the correct decision for both parties. The amount of stress and pressure I had been under over the past two years had affected my health and continued to do so long after I left the club. A month later, I left the training ground and drove down the M1 for the last time knowing that I would miss the players' camaraderie and banter but I also felt that a tremendous weight was immediately lifted off my shoulders.

While sitting down and writing my story I have had time to reflect on my career at Tottenham and these are some of my reflections:

1. I believe I gave the club seven years of hard work, with 100 per cent dedication at all times. My biggest achievement without doubt was getting Paul Gascoigne fit in the face of adversity when in reality he had no right to ever play football again at the highest level. This maybe helped solve some of the well-documented financial problems the club found themselves in at that time.

2. I proved that despite suffering from a disability you can work at the highest level in football medicine.

3. I believe I built an excellent relationship with players, staff and of course the supporters. We had a mutual respect and trust which enabled me to carry out my duties to the best of my ability.

4. I always regretted that we could not get the popular right-back Danny Thomas back to fitness after suffering an horrendous knee injury in a challenge with QPR's Gavin Maguire. As I watched the operation and discovered the extensive damage that he had suffered, I knew in my heart of hearts that it would be a miracle if Danny would ever play again. Surgeon John Browett worked long through the night and displayed all of his skill and expertise just to enable Danny to have a functional knee that would allow him to lead a normal life. Most of his rehabilitation was carried out at Headley Court and I will be eternally grateful to them for their time, patience, understanding and expertise. At that time a club physio would have found the task impossible.

5. A massive regret is being overlooked by Tottenham after going way beyond what could be reasonably expected of me. I put my life on hold for a year for the club and Paul during his rehabilitation, often to the detriment of my family. I didn't expect any monetary reward but it would have helped if somebody from the club took the time to ask if I was coping or if I needed support. I would have loved somebody to put their hand on my shoulder and say, 'How are you, John?' This time in my life affected my health for a long time afterwards and looking back I realise I suffered some sort of breakdown. But slowly with the love and care of my family I recovered to my old self and after a holiday in Majorca with Betty and Debbie I finally felt that I had my mojo back, ready to take on the world again. This was the period in football when mental health was swept under the carpet and observed as a weakness, but I would like to think that if the same situation arose today then the club would provide support mechanisms. Over the years the understanding and appreciation of mental health has improved, but it is important to remember that it is not just the players that suffer and I hope support is now provided for medical staff as well.

Ironically, not long after handing in my resignation letter, Terry was sacked due to a power struggle with chairman Alan Sugar. He did get reinstated after gaining a temporary injunction but was finally forced to leave the club after a High Court battle during the summer of 1993 when Sugar came out on top. Even though our relationship suffered a few ups and downs I did feel sorry for Terry. To his credit he stuck by me when he came in as manager in 1987. Sometimes he could be abrupt but underneath

I found him a loyal, thoughtful and caring man and to this day I still have the utmost respect for him.

In July 1993 I received a call from my old player at Tottenham, Ossie Ardiles, who had just taken over as manager of the club and asked if I would travel to White Hart Lane for a chat. I had always got on really well with Ossie and out of respect I agreed to meet him. It seemed strange going to the ground again such a short time after leaving, but I was looking forward to seeing him again. We hadn't seen each other since Ossie left the club in 1988 and he seemed delighted to see me again. Over the next hour or so he shared his plans for the club, which included my return as consultant physiotherapist with Danny Thomas potentially returning as first team physio. It was a great offer with a large pay rise compared to previously and the promise of new medical equipment. I didn't understand why they could offer this now and not before. I was tempted, mainly to work with this passionate Argentinian but with the bridges that had been burnt I knew it was now time to put my health and family first, so I sadly declined his offer. He also mentioned that he was going to sack my old assistant Dave Butler. I fought Dave's corner and told Ossie he had been a good assistant to me, but unfortunately Ossie was adamant that he was getting rid of him so he could bring in his own staff and have a fresh start.

I only returned to Spurs two more times. The first was shortly after the meeting with Ossie, when I was kindly invited to watch a home game and receive a present from the club. Just before the match the Tottenham assistant manager Steve Perryman presented me with some cut-glass crystal which I believe the players had clubbed together to buy me. I remember Teddy Sheringham asking me if I regretted leaving. I said to him, 'To be honest, Ted, I miss the players but not the club.'

The second and last time I visited White Hart Lane was in the early 2000s. David Pleat had returned to the club as director of football and I received a call from him saying, 'John, we are playing Newcastle United and Bobby Robson would like to see you again, he wondered if you would come to the game to see him?' I was delighted and immediately agreed. It was great to see Bobby again after all those years. We enjoyed a cup of coffee before the game and then had a long chat afterwards. I also met Ant and Dec who were there watching their beloved Newcastle and I must say that chairman Daniel Levy looked after me impeccably. For Sir Bobby to think of me and ask to see me again was extremely humbling and shows what a caring and thoughtful man he was.

13

A New Start

AFTER RECOVERING both physically and mentally from the last 18 months at Tottenham, I felt I was finally ready to move on and looked forward to a new chapter in my life. My clinic in Luton was now operating full time and was proving extremely popular among the local sportsmen and women. One of the main benefits of no longer working in professional football was the added time I could spend with my family at home. Gone were the days of spending countless nights away in soulless hotels up and down the country preparing for matches the following day. Club physiotherapists will understand that a career in professional football is not all glitz and glamour; you have to be a certain type of person to hold down this role for a prolonged period of time.

In the short spell since leaving the club I received a lot of phone calls and messages from people wanting to talk about why I walked away from a career in football. Some of them couldn't understand why I had left but the ones who really knew me said I had done the right thing. A close friend told me that he had seen an article in a tabloid newspaper which read, 'The real mystery is not how Paul Gascoigne managed to return to full fitness but why did physio John Sheridan leave Spurs while at the top of his profession.'

Even though I had no intention of going back to work in professional football, I still loved the game and would always look out for the results of Luton and Spurs. Over the years I have always kept in touch with David Pleat and it came as no surprise when he called me one morning in the summer of 1994, but it was a shock when he asked me if I would be interested in going back to Luton as consultant physio. David had recently returned as manager and offered me the chance to rejoin him in a part-time role supporting first-team physio Clive Goodyear. The position required me to work three mornings a week to treat any injuries and also attend first-team games at Kenilworth Road to assist with any problems on a matchday, so out of respect for David I promised I would think about the offer.

Even though my practice was thriving I had begun to miss the laughs and camaraderie of the players, and the chance to become consultant physio seemed to be the best of both worlds so after speaking to my family and getting their support I accepted but on the proviso that my private practice wouldn't be affected. From the first time I walked back into the treatment room at the famous old ground it felt as if I had never been away. The players and staff immediately made me feel extremely welcome and I thoroughly enjoyed being back among professional footballers and hearing the banter you will only find in a dressing room. The decision to return was definitely the right one and I enjoyed the mix of working in private practice and professional football. Sometimes instead of going to the club I would treat the injured Luton players in my clinic. Over the past few years I had saved some money, which enabled me to buy state of the art medical equipment and allowed me to give the lads a bit more time. They also enjoyed being outside of the club environment.

The Luton squad had a great mix of exciting young players including John Hartson, Paul Telfer and Tony Thorpe, and some fantastic experienced players such as David Preece, goalkeeper Marlon Beresford and midfielder Steve Robinson. I first met Steve in the early 1990s while he was an apprentice at Spurs, and he went on to have a good career at Bournemouth, Preston North End and Bristol City before joining Luton. From the first day I met Steve and his family we instantly enjoyed a trusting relationship, so much so that I continued to treat him throughout his career with the full knowledge of his clubs. Steve is a lovely, genuine man and I am delighted he has forged a successful career in management. To this day we are still great friends.

During my first year back at Luton an opportunity unexpectedly arose to return to the Premier League with Glenn Hoddle's Chelsea. We had always got on really well at Spurs and I was delighted to hear from him when he phoned me in early March 1995. Glenn told me that their physio Bob Ward had left to go to Middlesbrough and asked if I would be able to cover a couple of games for him. I told Glenn that I would love to help but as I was now working for Luton, I would have to ask David Pleat for permission. As usual David was great and fully appreciated Glenn's predicament, so he was more than happy for me to go to Chelsea for a short while. My first game was at home against Leeds on Saturday, 11 March, and I agreed to meet Glenn's assistant Peter Shreeves at 11am at Mill Hill services on the M1 so we could travel in together. The meeting time came and went but there was no sign of Peter, and I started to get a bit worried that I would be late for the game so at 11.30am I decided to leave the services and head towards Stamford Bridge by myself.

Luckily, the traffic was okay on my journey into west London and I arrived at the ground in plenty of time. I was shown to the treatment room and was met by midfielder Dennis Wise, who was waiting for me to treat him before the game. A short while later, Glenn popped in and asked if I had seen Peter. I explained that after waiting until 11.30am I couldn't afford to hang around any longer so I decided to make my own way to the ground. Glenn agreed this was the right thing to do and went off to carry on his search for his assistant manager, while I continued to get the players ready for the match.

Due to being so busy and enjoying the hurly-burly of a matchday, I didn't get a chance to give Peter another thought until shortly before kick-off. The door to the dressing room burst open and in walked a hot and bothered Peter, who turned to me and said, 'Where the fucking hell were you, John?' I replied, 'I was waiting at the entrance for you but when you didn't turn up, I thought I had better make my own way to the ground.' 'What fucking entrance were you waiting at?' he replied. 'How many are there?' I asked. Peter said, 'Obviously there must be two.' Trying not to laugh, I replied, 'Well I must have been waiting at the other one then!' Glenn and some of the other lads started to laugh and had to look away as Peter went on to say, 'You might think it's funny, there I was on the phone to your wife who told me you had left in plenty of time. Then to make matters worse somebody had reported me to the police as a suspicious person and they tried to arrest me!' To try and defuse the situation I said, 'Sorry, Peter, next time I will wait for you at the other entrance!' He smiled at me and started to laugh so I knew I had been forgiven.

It was fantastic to experience the matchday buzz and excitement at the top level again. The Chelsea dressing room ran like a well-oiled machine; everything the players might need was provided and it was a lot different to what I had experienced before but I loved every minute of it. Glenn's trusted ally, faith healer Eileen Drewery, was a member of the backroom team and was involved in the pre-match preparations as she helped the players who wanted guidance from her. Unfortunately the game didn't pan out as Glenn would have liked and we were well beaten by our opponents from Yorkshire, but I was pleased to renew my acquaintance with Geoff Ladley, the Leeds physio and my tutor from all those years ago at Lilleshall.

After making sure all of the players' knocks and injuries were taken care of, I was kindly invited to the directors' suite for a drink and felt privileged to meet the Chelsea vice-chairman Matthew Harding. He asked me, 'Did you enjoy the game and what are your thoughts of the medical department?' I replied, 'I have really enjoyed myself and am extremely impressed with the setup. Everyone had made me feel so welcome.' Tragically Matthew was killed in a helicopter crash on his way home after watching his beloved Chelsea play away at Bolton a little over 18 months later, when he was only 42 years old.

Over the years I have had the pleasure to meet a lot of the best players in England and I definitely had a few allies at Chelsea who would have put a good word in for me, especially Mark Stein who had been an apprentice during my first spell at Luton, and I was delighted he went on to be a prolific goalscorer at the highest level. Another ex-Luton player at Chelsea was Paul Elliott who was now a club ambassador, having been forced to retire from the game despite a long fitness battle after sustaining a serious knee injury in September 1992 from a challenge by Liverpool's Dean Saunders. I also remember having a nice chat with ex-Arsenal midfielder David Rocastle, who sadly died in 2001 after losing his brave battle with non-Hodgkin's lymphoma.

After such an enjoyable day at the club I was already looking forward to the next match on Tuesday, a quarter-final in the European Cup Winners' Cup at Stamford Bridge against Belgian side Club Brugge. Peter Shreeves and I decided that for this game we would travel in separately to avoid any more confusion! I arrived at the ground in the afternoon to be met with another new tracksuit and boots laid out for me, which was certainly a luxury and totally unexpected. Chelsea were 1-0 down from the first leg but their players were immense that night and won 2-0 thanks to goals from Mark Stein in the 16th minute and the tie-clincher from Paul Furlong shortly before half-time. The reward for this magnificent win was a place in the semi-final against Real Zaragoza.

The match against Club Brugge was televised live to the nation, although I wasn't aware of this at the time. A dear friend of mine called Rodney Blackman, who has sadly since passed away, was an avid Chelsea fan. I bumped into Rodney the day after the Leeds game and gave him a bit of stick about the result but without letting on I was the physio. You can imagine his surprise when he called me a couple of days after the Brugge match and said he almost had a heart attack as he watched a close-up on the TV of the bench and saw me sitting next to Glenn Hoddle in my new Chelsea tracksuit!

After the game, there was a tentative discussion regarding me joining the club in a permanent position and I would probably have grabbed it with both hands if I was a bit younger. But I enjoyed my new-found freedom and the part-time role at Luton suited me down to the ground. It allowed me to enjoy the banter associated with professional footballers and the excitement of matchdays but without the full-time commitment. Also, one of the most enjoyable parts of the job was helping and supporting physio Clive Goodyear, who had just recently qualified. He had welcomed me with open arms and I loved passing on some of my knowledge and experience.

Despite David Pleat leaving Luton in the summer of 1995 to take over at Sheffield Wednesday, I decided to stay on as consultant physiotherapist. Assistant manager Terry Westley was initially promoted to the top job but despite being a great coach it unfortunately didn't work out for him and he was replaced by the experienced Lennie Lawrence after six months. Lennie was a great person and manager and I thoroughly enjoyed my time while he was in charge. However, my private practice was going from strength to strength. I loved treating a different array of sportsmen and women which included Olympians, Paralympians and world championship boxers and I felt an immense sense of pride that I was able to help these elite athletes in a small way. Unfortunately, it got to a point where I couldn't realistically continue with both roles, so in 2000 I took the regrettable decision to leave Luton.

This wasn't, however, going to be the last time I had the pleasure to treat a professional footballer. I would regularly get calls from ex-players asking for treatment or a second opinion, and I was always happy to help as long as they had permission from the medical department at their club. Unfortunately, I did once get my fingers burnt. One morning I received a call from Teddy Sheringham who had been out injured for a while with a knee problem and was nowhere near to making a return. He asked if he could come to see me so I could have a look at his knee. I told him it would be fine to make sure that Ossie Ardiles and Spurs' medical staff knew about the visit. The next day

Teddy travelled from London to my house and after examining his knee I immediately suspected a meniscal tear and advised him to tell the medical staff at Tottenham he would require an arthroscopy to confirm my diagnosis. Teddy appreciated my advice and thanked me for seeing him before setting off back to the club. Within an hour of him leaving the phone in my clinic rang and I was met with an angry member of the Tottenham medical staff saying, 'How dare you look at one of my players, you don't know their medical history.' I assured him that I had only looked at Ted as I thought he had asked their permission but politely reminded him that as I had only just left the club, I was aware of the majority of Teddy's history. After putting the phone down, I quickly realised this was a lesson learned and promised myself that in the future I would always make sure to get permission first hand from the club's medical staff before agreeing to see another professional footballer.

Incidentally, I discovered Teddy did undergo an arthroscopy a couple of days later and it was discovered he had sustained a tear of the meniscus, but unsurprisingly I didn't receive a message from the club thanking me for the diagnosis, so when I received a call from Spurs winger Darren Anderton a week later asking to see me, I politely declined and advised him to speak to his own medical staff.

Another positive of being my own boss was I was now able to enjoy some well-earned holidays and trips away. Shortly before Gazza left Spurs for Lazio, he asked me if I would like to buy his camper van. He had bought it for his dad John to travel to Italy to visit him but I think he preferred flying to Rome so the van was surplus to requirements. Paul knew I had always wanted one and kindly let me have it for a great price. It had been hardly used and after a good service I became the proud owner of a Bursner motorhome that gave myself and my family many miles and hours of enjoyment.

This particular van had become famous within the Tottenham ranks as it was the same one that almost killed John Coberman. Gazza drove it into the training ground one day and for some reason asked John to get on the roof. As soon as he did Gazza decided to jump into the driver's seat and travel at high speed around the streets of Mill Hill with John holding on for dear life. When he eventually drove back into the training ground and parked up, John gingerly got off the roof and as he stepped off the last rung of the ladder he sunk to his knees and kissed the ground, thankful to be able to tell the tale.

14

Stories from Around the World

AFTER A long, hard season, the players and staff would look forward to an annual end-of-season trip abroad. There are many stories that I could talk about from our trips away with both Luton and Tottenham but unfortunately most of them aren't printable! I have been extremely fortunate to enjoy some great times and make so many unforgettable memories. While on these journeys, we would often meet up with other clubs who had the same idea. I have lost count of the amount of times I had the pleasure of enjoying an ice-cold beer or a glass of wine with some of the greatest managers and players in the world and would listen in awe as they recounted their experiences and stories of life in and out of football.

My first taste of a club trip abroad came with Luton Town at the end of the 1979/80 season. Our final game was away at Newcastle United, when the lads played well and earned a creditable 2-2 draw. As we travelled home everyone's thoughts focussed on the next day as we were due to fly to Spain for a week's rest and relaxation. The following morning the players and staff met bright and early at Kenilworth Road. As we boarded the coach for the journey to Heathrow it was clear to see the lads were looking forward to the break. There was a sense of excitement on the drive to the airport and as we arrived a few of the players had a quick lunchtime drink before the flight. David Pleat didn't come as I believe he was already planning for next season and had to tie up a couple of transfers. Therefore the responsibility was left to myself and assistant manager David Coates to look after the group throughout our time in Spain. As we walked up the steps to the plane myself and David had seats at the front while the lads stayed together near the back.

David was a big cricket fan and he quickly settled down for the flight by studying the cricket section of the *Daily Telegraph*. I was looking forward to taking off and heading towards the Spanish sun when all of a sudden I heard a commotion going on behind me. I looked round and was met with the sight of the co-pilot frog-marching two of our players towards the exit. David was still engrossed in his paper and seemingly had no idea what was going on so I got up and said, 'David, there seems to be a problem with a couple of the players but don't worry, I will go and sort it out.'

The co-pilot had marched them both off the plane so I followed them down the stairs to find out what had happened. The two players were a little bit worse for wear from the night before and I was told they had become a bit boisterous, so the stewardess reported them to the captain and he decided they would have to leave the plane. After much persuasion I managed to get one of the players back on board, but the co-pilot was adamant the other player was still too drunk to fly. He wouldn't be allowed back on board and would have to miss the trip. There was no way I could leave him on his own so we both made our way back to the terminal and watched the plane take off.

I was determined to somehow get to Spain and quickly realised I was faced with a dilemma; it was either no trip and hitch-hike back to Luton or think of a plan to get us out there. An idea quickly formed in my mind but to have any chance of catching another flight I had to somehow sober up my colleague. After plying him with endless black coffees, the effects of the alcohol started to wear off. I told him he would have to apologise to the airline and then say nothing and leave the talking to me. We went to see the duty manager of the airline, who luckily was a big football fan and instantly recognised the player and kindly accepted his apology. However, we were still stuck at the airport, which was when I put my plan into action. Lying through my teeth I said to the duty manager, 'I must apologise as I am partly to blame. The player is asthmatic and the mix of his medication and alcohol meant he has suffered a bad reaction. He is normally the politest person you are ever likely to meet and I'm sure he didn't mean to upset the stewardess. Is there any way we could get another flight to Spain as I am responsible for the players' welfare, their medication is on the plane and without me, there will be nobody to administer it.'

Luckily, he believed me and arranged for the pair of us to catch a direct flight to Palma which was due to take off shortly. To their credit the airline were magnificent, they treated us like VIPs and offered me free drinks throughout the flight. After boarding a plane for the second time that day I was ready for a drink but I looked at the player sitting alongside me – he was fast asleep, snoring with his head on the shoulder of the lady next to him. I was about to wake him up to get him to move but she put her finger to her mouth telling me to leave him sleeping!

The other plane with David Coates and the players on board had to stop at Barcelona where they would catch a connecting flight to Palma. Amazingly our flight was quicker, which meant we would get to the hotel before them. After a relaxing couple of hours on the plane we hired a taxi to the hotel. I made sure the player was okay before putting him to bed to sleep off his hangover. After organising the room keys for the rest of the players, I waited at the hotel bar for them to arrive. The look on their faces was priceless as they saw me in my shorts and sunglasses enjoying a nice cold beer! I was told later that day that David was so engrossed in his paper that he didn't realise I wasn't on the plane until halfway into the flight. Apparently, after one of the players told him what had happened, David calmly said, 'Don't worry, John will sort it out,' and he went back to reading the paper. We had a great trip that year and as ever David and the players were great company.

After returning from an end-of-season trip we would get the chance to enjoy a few well-earned weeks off with our families before returning back to work. Normally the first part of pre-season would be spent abroad for a training camp, and as you can imagine these were extremely hard work and completely different to the excursions that we enjoyed a few weeks before. However, I count myself lucky that I was able to travel to different parts of the world, taking in some stunning scenery and experiencing numerous different cultures. While with Luton we would often visit Scandinavian countries to play against their local sides and were always treated exceptionally well. These trips enabled us to meet some fantastic people and make numerous new Luton fans.

The Middle East was another favourite place for us to visit, I suppose to help raise some much-needed funds for the club. One particular trip springs to mind. We had just won the Second Division title and as a thank you we flew to Saudi Arabia in May 1982. We enjoyed a couple of days' rest before playing a scheduled match against a Saudi league team at the local athletics stadium. The heat and humidity as we kicked off the game was horrific; I was sweating just sitting on the bench so I dread to think how bad it was for the players. Half-time came and we were pleased to get into the sanctuary of the air-conditioned dressing room. Normally the referee would sound a bell for us to leave the dressing room for the start of the second half, but on this occasion the half-time break seemed to go on for ever. I was worried as we were due to fly to Bahrain shortly after the final whistle, so I decided to find out what was causing the delay.

To my astonishment I was told the second half couldn't restart as the athletics track was being used for a race and the game wouldn't start until it had finished. I managed to find a club official and told him that unless we kicked off soon, we would miss our flight. Coolly, he said to me, 'Don't worry, you are guests of Saudi Arabia, I will call the airline and tell them that the plane cannot take off until you are on board.' The second half eventually restarted but unfortunately the heat and humidity hadn't subsided, some of the players were really struggling with dehydration and we were all relieved to hear the final whistle. We returned to the dressing room to cool down and I made sure the players rehydrated by drinking as much as possible. Even though the plane had been delayed on our behalf we still made a mad dash to the airport. As we boarded, myself and David Moss carried one of the players on our shoulders as he was still suffering from the effects of dehydration. After the short flight to Bahrain we were relieved to check in to a luxury hotel, and some of the players went off to the bar to enjoy a well-earned beer. However, one of the lads still hadn't recovered fully and I was becoming increasingly concerned about his health, so I left the rest of the group at the hotel and rushed him to hospital. It was the correct decision as he was admitted and placed on a drip for the night to help him rehydrate.

I remember this trip vividly because of a magnificent feast hosted by the government and the prince of Bahrain. I had the pleasure of sitting next to the prince throughout the banquet and the hospitality and kindness that was shown to us throughout our stay was second to none. During the trip I was approached by a local official in Dhahran asking if I would be interested in becoming the full-time physiotherapist for their local club. I was given a tour around their stadium and was amazed to see some of the most up-to-date medical equipment, which was unbelievably still in its original packaging and unused. Despite the kind offer I decided to turn it down as I was happy at Luton and more importantly it wasn't right for my family.

A couple of years after joining Luton, I was fortunate enough to go on an end-of-season trip to Fort Lauderdale in America. My room-mate for the two-week break was Dr Bill Berry. One morning after breakfast, myself, Bill and our skilful winger David Moss went for a walk around the local shopping centre. Naturally we made a beeline for the first sports shop and I was amazed to discover they stocked everything you could think of, but I was especially intrigued by a stand displaying sports supports. I had never seen these before so I asked the manager for more information. He told me they were a new product on the market and had become very popular. The supports were made of neoprene and were extremely durable and retained flexibility over a wide range of temperatures but most importantly gave good support. If we could somehow get them in England, they would save the club a considerable amount of money as they could be washed and reused over a long period of time while maintaining the same level of support.

I asked the store manager if it was possible to export them to me when I got back to the club, which he could do, but he suggested because they were so well liked it could be a good opportunity to set up a franchise to sell them back in the UK. After speaking with Bill and David we were definitely interested and decided to trial them first before we committed to a franchise. Before returning to England, I bought enough to get us started. As soon as I introduced the supports at the club the players loved them, especially the ankle supports which were extremely good. So after a short trial myself, Bill, Mossy and an avid Luton fan called Derek Filmer made the decision to set up a company to start selling them in the UK. Despite the strappings selling extremely well, it soon became apparent that after the cost of importing them and paying the relevant taxes there was very little profit left over.

Undeterred, we knew the potential of this type of support so decided to explore the possibility of making them ourselves in this country. After numerous meetings with rubber companies and designers we came to the heartbreaking decision that we just couldn't fund the project. Unfortunately the massive outlay of producing machinery, material costs and premises just proved too much. We continued to import the supports from America for a short while but that eventually fizzled out due to a lack of time and money. These supports have now become extremely popular and you can buy them in most good sports shops, chemists and even supermarkets. It was a shame as with a little bit of luck and money we could have led the way in sports supports. As Del Boy would say, 'This time next year we could be millionaires!'

On Sunday, 12 May 1985 I flew out to Cyprus with the rest of the Luton squad and assistant manager Trevor Hartley.

We had just beaten Leicester City 4-0 at Kenilworth Road the previous day and even though there were still two games remaining of the season, our next one wasn't until 23 May. I believe David Pleat organised this trip for two reasons. The first was that we had enjoyed a good season and were guaranteed a mid-table finish. The second was to help morale after we had been beaten 2-1 in extra time a few weeks earlier in the FA Cup semi-final against Everton at Villa Park. The disappointment after this match remains the biggest I have ever felt after a game of football, including losing the 1987 FA Cup Final with Tottenham against Coventry. Instead of walking out under the famous Wembley twin towers to face Ron Atkinson's Manchester United team we would be watching the 1985 final in Limassol with a beer in our hands thinking that with a little bit of luck it could have been us.

After landing at Limassol Airport, we made our way to a comfortable but basic hotel that was to be our home for the next week. A few days into our trip we were due to play against a local side called Apollon FC at their Tsirion Stadium. The day of the match arrived and due to a food bug, we only had ten fit players. To make up the 11th man it was going to be a toss up between myself, the ex-Taverners goalkeeper who played a handful of games before graciously retiring for a career in physiotherapy, or Trevor Hartley, the ex-West Ham and Bournemouth midfielder. So Trevor came out of retirement and took his place on the pitch at the heart of the defence alongside club legend Mick Harford. The dynamic duo were magnificent for 90 minutes; Mick was his usual superb competitive self and Trevor played out of his skin. He must have been some player in his prime. As I was the only person from the club on the touchline, for one night only I had been promoted to the role of manager as well as physio and substitute. It was an enjoyable match that if I remember correctly finished in a creditable draw. Apollon included a guest player for the game, the one and only George Best, and it was a pleasure to watch him play.

During the match I had a good chat with Apollon's manager. We talked about the players and one in particular, as he asked, 'Who is the little blonde central defender? I am really impressed with him, he is technically very good and would fit in to our team. Is he for sale?' Somehow I kept a straight face and said, 'Everyone is available for the right price. Trevor has a good couple of years left in him and I think he would be interested in a move. If you make me an offer I will speak to the chairman and see if we can put a deal together.' He walked away happy that there might be a chance to make a star signing for the coming season. The final whistle went so we headed back to the dressing room, and as I was manager for the evening I pretended to give a team talk. Trevor was still breathing out of his arse as I announced that I had sold him to Apollon. The look on his face was priceless as he gave a half-hearted smile through clenched teeth. The lads gave him a bit of stick and I knew it was just a matter of time before he would try and get his own back.

The next morning myself and Trevor headed out of our basic hotel for a walk along the seafront. I promised I would buy him a coffee to make up for trying to sell him the previous day, so we decided to go for a drink at a nearby five-star hotel. As we sat down for our expensive coffee we looked on in awe at the plush surroundings and beautiful swimming pool, which were very different to the three-star hotel that the club had booked for us to stay in. We looked at each other and immediately knew what we were thinking, so we thought of a plan to get past the security guards and enjoy the luxury. We decided to be brazen and bluff our way in by pretending to be residents, so after finishing our coffees we placed a newspaper under our arms and walked casually to the entrance of the complex. We greeted the security guards like long-lost friends and they politely let us through. What a result; for the next few days we would get up early, leave the budget hotel behind us and make our way to enjoy the plush trappings of the nearby hotel. By the time we strolled back each evening feeling refreshed the players asked us where we had been all day. We tried to keep our hotel swap a secret but a couple of the lads guessed what we were up to. One morning they followed us and without a second thought the pair of them walked into the posh hotel to join us by the pool.

After enjoying a relaxing week, we flew back into Luton Airport with morale restored and ready for the final two matches of the season. Unfortunately we lost the first of those, 1-0 away to Coventry, in a hard-fought battle. However, our final game was at home to Everton and all of the players, staff and supporters were desperate to gain some revenge for the recent semi-final defeat. The atmosphere at Kenilworth Road was electric, the fans and players were superb and we beat them comfortably 2-0 through goals from Emeka Nwajiobi and Ricky Hill.

I had one more season at Luton before myself, Trevor and David Pleat moved to Spurs. It was shortly into the first campaign at our new club when Trevor eventually got his own back on me. During an international break we travelled to Trinidad and Tobago for four days which included three friendly matches against some of our English counterparts. David had stayed at home to concentrate on the day-to-day running of the club so it was left to myself and Trevor to look after the players. I had been at Spurs since July and started to form some good relationships with them. Just before a game against Norwich City, the lads lined up as the squads were announced over the PA system. After all the Spurs players were read out to the crowd it was then myself and Trevor's turn, so he continued, 'The coach for tonight's game is Trevor Hartley and the physio is Sir John Sheridan MBE, CBE, OBE.' The players turned to look at me not knowing whether to laugh or cry and wondering if they would have to bow before receiving treatment. It wasn't just the Spurs players looking at me, I felt as if I had the eyes of the Norwich staff and all the supporters in the ground bearing down on me. Trevor looked over at me, gave me a big smile and a wink. He had his revenge!

At the end of the same season we travelled to Florida for a ten-day break. David had arranged for us to play one of the South American countries in the Orange Bowl Stadium, which was the home of the famous NFL team Miami Dolphins until it closed in 2008. I think the friendly was against Chile but after all these years and thousands of games I can't be 100 per cent sure, but the real reason for remembering this trip is a painful one.

The day before the game the players had a light training session at our hotel. Just before the lads came out, I took up my normal position by the side of the pitch. A short while after the session started, Chris Waddle was positioned close to the touchline as somebody clipped him a lovely pass to hit on the volley. Unfortunately for me his wand of a left foot let him down, he slightly mis-hit it and from a distance of approximately ten yards I felt the full force of the ball as it struck me in the unmentionables. I felt as if I had been hit by a steam train, the air was instantly expelled out of my lungs and the only sound I could make was a loud URGHHH!

Although my wedding tackle was in extreme pain, I somehow still had my pride intact as I managed to stay on my feet. With tears in his eyes, Chris walked over to me and said, 'Are you all right, John? Sorry, it was a complete accident.' With my voice a few octaves higher I replied, 'I think so.' To try and hide my blushes I slowly walked off to the toilet and threw up. After composing myself and making a slight recovery I walked slowly and gingerly back to the pitch. A couple of the lads were still creased up in laughter, so I said to them, 'If it had happened to one of you, you would have been rolling around on the floor in agony begging for me to treat you.'

Chris left Tottenham to move to Marseille in 1989 then returned to England a couple of years later with Sheffield Wednesday, and whenever I would bump into him, without fail the first thing he would say to me was 'URGHHH' before laughing and then enjoying a chat.

15

Matchdays

I ALWAYS looked forward to matchdays, particularly on a Saturday. The buzz and excitement started on a Friday when the players would have a light training session in the morning, then after chatting with myself and the coaches the manager would name the squad for the following day. After a spot of lunch, the lads would go home and then the preparations began in earnest. The apprentices would come in to clean the treatment room and both dressing rooms from top to bottom. I often thought these boys were glorified cleaners but they absolutely loved being involved with the senior players.

I had to make sure the medical equipment was prepared but just as important the ice machine was stocked up with beer for the opposition staff. The kit was laid out immaculately by the kit man and also the boots were polished and put on their pegs ready for the next day. If our opposition had travelled a long distance and were staying in a local hotel, their physio and kit man would often turn up on a Friday afternoon to prepare the dressing room. After they had finished the door would be locked and they would keep the key until after the game so nothing could be sabotaged.

Once, a famous manager turned up with his staff to inspect our facilities. He left no stone unturned as he checked the dressing room, showers, bath and toilets. Looking back now, that memory reminds me of the TV series *Four in a Bed*. I imagine these are the marks he would have given us:

Hosting Skills
Both Luton and Spurs were renowned for always being good hosts. **Score: 10**

Cleanliness
After running his finger across the door frames and finding some dust and cobwebs, the apprentices were summoned to do a deep clean. **Score: 7**

Facilities
You cannot make a silk purse out of a sow's ear. Kenilworth Road is an old stadium steeped in tradition but during my first spell at the club the dressing rooms and facilities definitely needed updating. **Score: 6**

Sleep Quality
On numerous occasions we have caught the opponents' defence napping so must be a **10!**

Breakfast
This was usually a late breakfast as sandwiches were provided after the game. They were always of a high quality and presented impeccably on a silver tray. However, it has been known on occasions for the tray to go flying towards a player after a bad performance often requiring a few stitches. So, a score of **10** is awarded for both the quality of sandwiches and also the manager's aim.

Would you come here again?
This depended on if you were promoted or relegated, of course.

After a long trip to an away game I always found it relaxing to go to the opposition's ground to prepare for the next day. In my first year at Luton I would have to do the lot, but throughout the remainder of my career I had the luxury of a kit man. The physio and the kit man usually got on really well and I was lucky enough to have a great relationship with firstly George Rogers, and then at Spurs with Roy Reyland. Whenever possible we would help each other out, especially with the skips which were extremely heavy. After a game I would make sure all the injured players were okay then help pack the skips before having a quick shower. If there was enough time left, I would sit down with the opposition manager, physio and coaching staff for a quick drink. Occasionally, if we had suffered a bad result the manager would say to the players and staff 'straight on the coach' and you would be struggling to get everything done in time. I have heard of more than one occasion when a physio has been left behind after the coach has departed and has had to find his own way home. This happened to a fellow physio who was employed by a club located in London. They had played a northern team and after being left stranded at the ground he found himself walking across Victoria Station in the early hours of the morning in his tracksuit and holding his bucket and sponge.

Every player has their own routines and superstitions on a matchday, whether that be putting on a certain sock before the other or having to walk out last from the tunnel. They also had routines within the treatment room such as what time they get their massage or when they get their wedding ring taped up. Gary Lineker had an unusual way of preparing himself for a match; he would often have a quick dip in a warm bath as he believed it would relax his muscles. As soon as he got out, I would have to stop what I was doing and immediately strap his ankles before he would get changed. I remember one game against Manchester City at White Hart Lane when Gazza decided that if it was good enough for Gary then it would be good enough for him. Gary had just finished his bath when Gazza jumped in and stayed in there for a lot longer than he should have done and unfortunately when he eventually decided to get out, he was bright red, exhausted and could hardly walk. It didn't bode well as within 15 minutes we were 2-0 down. That was the last time he had a bath before a game.

A matchday that will always stick in my mind is Saturday, 1 November 1986 against Wimbledon at White Hart Lane. This day was the closest I have ever been to getting sent off. It was a particularly bad-tempered clash against a team that included the likes of John Fashanu, Brian Gayle and Vinny Jones. Shortly before half-time our right-back Gary Stevens sustained a serious shoulder injury while attempting to stop the opening goal and was forced to go off. David Pleat reorganised the side during the break but in the second half Graham Roberts tussled with Wimbledon's Lawrie Sanchez and went down injured. After assessing him, I realised he could no longer play any part and due to the serious nature of his injury I decided he needed to be stretchered off. As I walked alongside a motionless Graham, the notorious referee David Axcell came over and sent Graham off. I reacted angrily and said, 'Referee, don't be stupid, you can't do that. He is injured and going off anyway.' In no uncertain terms he told me, 'Physio, shut up or I will send you off as well.' Years later I was playing *Trivial Pursuit* with the family and one of the questions was, 'Which footballer was sent off while lying injured on a stretcher?' At least I got that one right.

The game was a typical bruising encounter against Wimbledon, but revenge was sweet as on 15 March 1987 we managed to beat them 2-0 in the FA Cup quarter-final thanks to late goals from Chris Waddle and a superb long-range free kick from Glenn Hoddle. The reward for this hard-fought win was a place in the semi-final at Villa Park against Graham Taylor's Watford.

A couple of years later, the rivalry between the two clubs spilled over again which unfortunately resulted in another serious injury to Gary Stevens. During a league game at White Hart Lane in November 1988, Gary was shielding the ball from John Fashanu when out of nowhere Vinny Jones came flying in with an unnecessary sliding tackle that resulted in him sustaining a nasty knee injury. After examining him I quickly realised the severity of the injury. The tackle was needless and I was fuming that history had seemingly just repeated itself and Gary was again faced with another lengthy spell out of the game.

As I left the field with Gary on a stretcher, I told Vinny what I thought of him and my emotions were still running high as we approached the dugouts, so I decided to give the Wimbledon bench – which included manager Bobby Gould and Don Howe – both barrels. This was completely out of character for me. I pride myself on keeping my cool but on this occasion my passion for the players' welfare led me to say something I shouldn't have. We managed to win the game 3-2 thanks to rare goals from Guy Butters, Terry Fenwick and Vinny Samways but at the final whistle there was still some bad feeling simmering between myself and the Wimbledon bench. As we headed up the tunnel the argument continued and there was an angry confrontation about my defamatory comments aimed towards them. For those of you who know the old White Hart Lane ground the press box, which was full of reporters at the time, overlooks the dugouts and unfortunately they witnessed the entire episode.

After sorting out the knocks and injuries, I got showered and changed and thought no more of what had happened. As I was just about to leave the dressing room Terry Venables came in looking for me and said, 'John, you have been reported to the FA over your remarks to the Wimbledon staff. The press are outside waiting for a comment so be careful what you say,' and with that he shot off and left me to it. A moment later there was a knock at the door and in walked a reporter I trusted and had known for a number of years. He said, 'John, I will tell you what to say to get you out of the crap, they don't want to get you into trouble but will crucify you if you say the wrong thing.' After taking his advice I headed out to see the waiting press and apologised for any comments that might have offended anyone. This seemed to do the trick and defused the situation. The following week I was told the FA would take no further action due to my unblemished record. I was always fiercely protective about all of my players and even all these years later I would probably do the same thing again. I have seen Vinny Jones on the golf course a few times over the years and we have always given a friendly wave to each other. Without doubt the Crazy Gang added something to football back then and despite the physical nature of their approach to football the game wouldn't have been as colourful without them.

Sometimes matchday travel is as memorable as the game itself. One such incident happened early on in my career at

Spurs, when during a short break in the season we had to make a day trip to Northern Ireland to play in a testimonial at the famous old Windsor Park ground. The Troubles were coming to an end and the players were looking forward to playing in front of the passionate Irish supporters. The plan for the day was a quick flight over the Irish Sea, play the game, enjoy a little bit of hospitality then fly back home. Before we set off from White Hart Lane, I was warned not to take too much medical equipment as there wasn't going to be much room on the plane.

We arrived at Luton Airport and after making our way through passport control we walked out on to the tarmac to be greeted by a pair of eight-seater propeller aeroplanes that were so old they looked as if they had been used in the Second World War. The squad split into two and took their places on the clapped-out planes. Seats were at a premium and as one of the senior members of the group I had the pleasure of sitting next to the pilot. As we taxied along the runway, he turned to me and said, 'John, you are now the co-pilot so please keep an eye out your side, as you never know what might appear!'

The outward flight was non-eventful and we enjoyed the sun and lovely views over the Irish Sea. After landing at Belfast Airport we made the short trip to Windsor Park. The game was played in front of a passionate sell-out crowd and throughout our stay everyone made us feel most welcome. After enjoying a few refreshments after the game, we were whisked off back to the airport to start our short flight home. Even though the planes weren't the most comfortable the atmosphere on board was jovial as we headed back to England. Halfway across the Irish Sea the fog started rolling in and visibility became extremely poor, so the atmosphere among the players started to change and there were a few worried faces behind me.

Over the next few minutes we were told by air traffic control that Luton was fog-bound so we would have to divert to Stansted, and then that Stansted was also fog-bound so we would instead have to go to East Midlands Airport. The lads could hear these messages and some looked extremely worried as all we could see out of the window was thick fog. Their mood wasn't helped when the pilot muttered, 'Because of the diversions we have used more fuel; if we don't land soon we will run out.' Somehow we managed to get to East Midlands on fumes and as the wheels touched the runway there was a huge sigh of relief from all on board.

16

Injury Management, Assessment and Rehabilitation

OVER FIVE decades I am pleased to say the treatment room and electrotherapy equipment has evolved and improved alongside the way a therapist approaches and treats an injury. From my early years I can remember the old heat lamp and therapists digging their thumbs into an injury with the old adage 'no pain no gain'.

When I first joined Luton Town, the treatment room was old-fashioned but clean and the electrotherapy equipment had seen better days. My first job was to get everything tested to make sure it was safe to use and working correctly, as it had been known for Football League clubs to regularly use their electrotherapy equipment without it actually working correctly or even operating at all. One of our directors, Terry Bailey, kindly revamped the treatment room a couple of years later with brand new cupboards and surfaces from his company, Wallspan Bedrooms. This support allowed me to improve the environment but the biggest help was from the fans, who helped raise money for new electrotherapy and exercise equipment that gave the club some of the most up-to-date facilities of that era.

When I moved to Tottenham, I was pleasantly surprised with the level of equipment at both the Cheshunt training ground and also in the treatment room at White Hart Lane. There was, however, still room for improvement and during the first couple of years the club allowed me to invest in some excellent electrotherapy and gym equipment. One of the most important purchases of that time was the Cybex isokinetic machine and computer, which allowed me to rehabilitate to exact parameters. To my knowledge we were the first league club to install this cutting-edge piece of equipment and although it did cost a lot of money, it repaid the club ten-fold by enabling the players to return to fitness earlier. Although electrotherapy equipment played an integral part in the rehabilitation process, my emphasis was on remedial exercises. This type of rehab alongside hydrotherapy was my major weapon in getting a player back ready for training and matches.

No club physiotherapist would be able to do their job to the best of their ability without a comprehensive support network behind them. This would generally include the local hospital, chiropodist, dentist, chaplain and optician. The club doctor would also play an important part in the day-to-day running of a medical department, and I certainly count myself lucky to have had the support of Dr Berry at Luton then, after a sticky start, Dr Curtin at Tottenham was a fantastic ally. The local chemist and medical suppliers were an integral part of the team, so it was always important to make sure they were paid on time. It was always imperative for a physio to have a good knowledge of medication as often you were on your own when travelling away from home or abroad. The goodwill of many people is required to assist you, especially on a matchday when St John Ambulance and paramedics were in attendance. Last but not least you would have to be aware of the protocols of the drug testers. We had two occasions, one at Luton and one at Tottenham, when the two players picked for testing had been sent off for fighting each other. After the game ended, they would be in the treatment room eyeing each other up and it would just be a matter of time before it kicked off again, but despite a few verbals they would generally make up as off the field most players were mates.

To help in the management and rehabilitation of an injury to a professional sportsman, it is important to enjoy a trusting relationship between the physio and player. Sometimes this meant being more than just a physio and due to the accident in my teens I have first-hand experience of how it feels to have to fight back from a serious injury. This enabled me to show genuine compassion and a sixth sense to understand how an injured player was feeling. Did they need to be worked hard or just need an arm round their shoulder and a trusting ear to listen to their feelings and concerns? I often found the best way to get them, injured or not, to tell you their worries was to take some time out of the football environment. At Tottenham a favourite way of mine to do this was to take the player to the local pitch and putt golf course in Mill Hill where they would normally open up and tell me their concerns. Doing this type of thing can only deepen the relationship and because of this philosophy there have been players I have looked after and advised throughout their careers as they knew they could trust me 100 per cent. Psychology plays a major part in the treatment room and you must know your players. When doing rehabilitation, it is important to try and have a really optimistic-minded player because without doubt he will lift the other lads around him, make your day flow and help create a positive environment.

An injury to the talented midfielder Lil Fuccillo during my first year at Luton taught me a valuable lesson in the rehabilitation process of a broken leg. He had sustained the injury at Brighton & Hove Albion on 16 December 1978. After I joined the club in July 1979, I discovered Lil had been given the green light to resume training. He had been x-rayed to confirm that the fracture had healed and the consultant was pleased with his progress, so was happy for him to return. Lil trained with the first team and showed no signs of concern and as part of his comeback a friendly was arranged against the youth team. During this friendly he was involved in a nasty tackle which resulted in him re-fracturing the same leg in the same place. Both myself and Lil were distraught. Further tests showed there had been a partial non-union, and excess callus around the original fracture had formed which was the reason the consultant had unknowingly given a false diagnosis. We were back to square one, but due to Lil's hard work and after extensive rehabilitation he made a full recovery and regained his place at the heart of the Luton midfield. He went on to play a major part in the promotion season of 1981/82. Lil left that summer for a move to Tulsa Roughnecks in the North American Soccer League, but returned to England the same year and went on to play for teams such as Southend United, Peterborough United and Cambridge United.

Lil's misfortune highlighted that a fracture site is vulnerable for a period of time after the fracture is thought to have healed. When he made his second comeback, I wanted to add some extra protection for the original injury so I arranged with the Luton and Dunstable Hospital for them to make a lightweight splint which was moulded to the contours of his lower leg and was worn under the normal shin pad. This worked well and I believe it added a psychological edge for Lil as he felt wearing it provided extra reassurance that he would be okay. The wearing of a tailored splint for an individual player after a fracture was a practice I continued throughout my career. Although it was rare for a player to sustain the same fracture during his comeback, I definitely believe it was better to be safe instead of taking any risks, which was proved right when I received a phone call one morning from a player. After recently returning from a fractured tibia he had just transferred from Luton to a fellow First Division club. During his first match for the new team he was on the receiving end of a particularly dangerous, over-the-ball tackle. Luckily the result was only a bruised shin but it completely shattered the protective splint. He phoned to thank me for getting the splint made and said if he hadn't worn it, he would have faced another lengthy spell out of the game.

The management of head injuries in football is a hot topic. Recent studies have discovered high rates of concussion and a serious brain disorder called chronic traumatic encephalopathy (CTE). This type of dementia does not respect or discriminate whether you are a footballing great, a journeyman or just a humble player who played for the love of the game. Many years before, I remember sitting entranced at Lilleshall while listening to a lecture from a softly spoken Scottish neurosurgeon called Myles Gibson. Mr Gibson described in detail the importance of correct management of head injuries while on the field of play and emphasised that this type of injury must be treated with the utmost caution and no chances should be taken. I wonder all these years later if he knew what the consequence would be of heading a football, repeated blows to the head and concussion over a period of years for some of our players of times gone by. It is so sad to see some of these men lose their mental faculties and sometimes pass away at such a young age when they have so much to look forward to. At last this type of dementia is

Staying calm whilst treating Gary Mabbutt for a serious head injury

Running on at Anfield

Myself and Terry concentrating on the match, not sure what assistant manager Allan Harris has seen!

Gazza's tackle on Gary Charles that changed my life

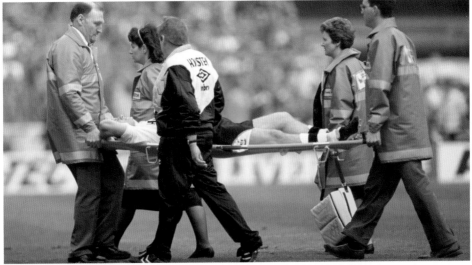

Gazza's dream transfer to Lazio seems a long way away as I walk alongside him off the Wembley pitch

Brigitte Nielsen trying Gazza's crutches in Portugal!

Chasing Gazza with the famous shark. That will teach him for putting me in the crow's nest!

Almost there! Working hard with Gazza

He's back!! Scoring one of his goals in a 4-2 victory v Spurs reserves. I am looking on in the background trying to stay dry!

Gazza under the watchful eye of Jim Andrews in Rome

We did it! Gazza is officially a Lazio player. You can see on my face that I am totally exhausted and just want to get home!

Pen picture at Spurs (early 1990s)

A moving article from Gazza

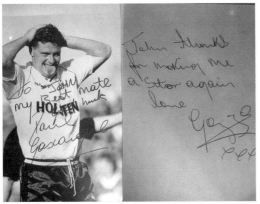

A lovely tribute from Gazza 'John thanks for making me a star again'

Receiving a present from Steve Perryman on behalf of the players and staff in 1993

Enjoying a Q&A session with the Malta Supporters Club.

My private practice in Luton. Proudly hanging on the wall are some of the shirts I have been kindly given by players over the years

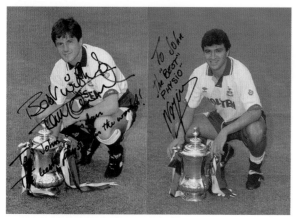

A couple of lovely messages from Terry Fenwick and Nayim

Treating Ian Hendon whilst kitman Roy Reyland looks on

Relaxing with Ossie Ardiles and the late, great Ray Clemence whilst on an end of season break

Off to Florida to enjoy a mid-season break with Spurs

Looking concerned! (right to left – myself, Roy Reyland, Allan Harris and Terry Venables)

Semi-final joy at the final whistle

With Brian Stein, Vera Antic, the late great Raddy Antic, Trevor Hartley & Steve White

Sharing a joke with David Pleat and Brian 'Nobby' Horton

Enjoying a game of golf with my great friend Sam Hill

Luton Irish Golf Society captains Weekend (Jolly Boys' Outing!)

One of my all-time favourite players – Nayim – A real gentleman

My beloved children Andy, Debbie and Paul

recognised as an industrial injury, so hopefully with increased awareness and research funded by the FA and PFA the players and families who are presently suffering can get support and just as important the future players can be spared from this dreadful disease.

The pressures physiotherapists can be under while treating a head injury can be immense. The crowd are baying at you to get off the pitch and also the referee may be hurrying you up but the biggest issue can be from the players themselves. During my career there were occasions when a player would argue with me that they were fine and wanted to stay on. They didn't want to let their team-mates down, especially in the era of only one permitted substitute. One incident happened during a Luton Town v Tottenham Hotspur match at Kenilworth Road when Spurs right-back Gary Stevens went down after a collision. After assessing him I suspected he had been knocked out and was suffering from concussion. I told Gary he was coming off immediately but he was desperate to continue playing and became aggressive, which was unlike him. Despite Gary's desire to stay on, the substitution was made and I escorted him off the pitch. The philosophy of taking no chances proved correct, as shortly after we returned to the changing room he collapsed before being examined by the doctor.

One of the first head injuries I had to deal with in professional football happened in a game between Luton and Leicester City in the late 1970s at the Foxes' famous old Filbert Street ground. This one springs to mind as it was the first time I ran on to the pitch and treated a player in front of the television cameras. Our goalkeeper Jake Findlay ended up flat on his back after sustaining a head injury, having collided with an opponent's knee. The referee immediately realised the seriousness of the situation and called me on, even before I had time to reach the touchline. Luckily the injury wasn't as bad as first feared and after treating Jake and getting him checked by the club doctor, he was able to continue for the remainder of the game. As I sat down to watch *Match of the Day* that evening I suddenly started to wonder if my treatment of him would be analysed by the millions of armchair critics. The footage of the incident was played and I was pleased to watch as my strict first aid training had kicked in while looking after Jake.

Throughout my decades in football I have had to deal with some very nasty injuries but I can honestly say one of the worst was a facial injury to Terry Butcher. Luton were playing Ipswich Town in the FA Cup at Kenilworth Road in January 1982, and during the game Brian Stein accidentally kicked Butcher, the uncompromising England defender, in the face. Terry suffered a serious nosebleed and myself and Dr Berry spent over an hour trying to stop the flow of blood, which could have easily ended in tragedy for the player. Unfortunately he couldn't be transferred to hospital until we had stabilised him and an extremely worried Bobby Robson kept coming into the treatment room to see how we were coping. Eventually we managed to get him in a condition where he was able to travel to hospital, but I understand they struggled to control the flow of blood as the bleeding would keep stopping and starting. During Terry's stay in hospital it was discovered that he had ruptured one of the nasal arteries that supplies the nose with a rich vascular supply of blood. Terry spent five weeks in hospital, lost a stone and a half in weight and had 19 units of blood transfused, which saved his life. I later read that while receiving treatment he was given a handkerchief from a faith healer who told him to put it on his nose and the bleeding would stop – and apparently it did! But I would like to think the Luton medical staff were there for him when he needed it most.

Another extremely serious facial injury happened during a game for Tottenham. We were playing at White Hart Lane against Howard Wilkinson's title-challenging Leeds United when centre-forward Lee Chapman and Spurs defender Steve Sedgley went for the same ball as it headed out of play near the touchline. Somehow Lee ended up sliding face-first on the cinder track that surrounded the pitch, which resulted in him sustaining numerous large cuts on his face. I immediately escorted him to the treatment room where myself and Dr Curtin found ourselves picking grit out of the cuts on his bloodied face, then cleaning him with antiseptic solution before a dressing was applied to lessen the risk of infection. Lee was then taken to hospital and required plastic surgery and many stitches to repair the damage to his face. Spurs received a very nice letter from Howard Wilkinson thanking the club's medical staff for looking after Lee in very difficult circumstances.

One of the most rewarding parts of the role of a physio is when against all odds you get a player fit for a big game. In 1988, after I had joined Spurs, I got a phone call from one of my old Luton players, Ricky Hill, shortly before their League Cup Final against Arsenal. Ricky had broken his leg and badly damaged ankle ligaments in a challenge on Boxing Day 1987 against Everton, but despite recovering from the broken leg he was still struggling with his ankle and was worried he would miss one of the biggest matches in the club's history. In the build-up to the final, Ricky came to my home in Luton for treatment and I am pleased to say he recovered and played the whole game in front of almost 96,000 people as my old club recorded a magnificent 3-2 victory over Arsenal. I assumed that Luton knew he was coming to see me but I thought we had managed to keep it quiet from everyone else – apart from Terry Venables, who came into the treatment room at Mill Hill shortly after the final and asked if I had treated any Luton players recently. I didn't say a word and instead just nodded. There are no secrets in football.

Due to the stresses and strains of managers and supporters wanting to win each week, the majority of a physio's remedial work is to get a player fit to return to playing as soon as possible. However, I have always believed that you have a duty of care to look after your player's long-term health as well, which would sometimes mean stopping them playing in a game even if they felt fit enough to play. In my first season at Spurs a player had a slight hamstring strain, so I told the manager he couldn't play on a Tuesday night in the League Cup but would be okay for the next match on Saturday in the league. The player was fuming and stormed off to speak to David Pleat, who as ever backed me 100 per cent. This particular player didn't take the news too well as at the time he was having a great season.

The following day the squad reported for the cup game and uncharacteristically Gary Mabbutt didn't turn up, so this player had to be named on the bench. Due to other injuries he actually came on with ten minutes to go and didn't look right, then after the game he came to see me and said, 'Sorry, John, you were right. I did feel the injury.' I appreciated his honesty and apology.

Despite what happened, the priority was to find out what had happened to Gary. I believe it was Ossie Ardiles who sounded the warning and luckily had the phone number of Gary's neighbour. With no answer at the house the neighbour called the police, who broke in and found Gary unconscious in a diabetic coma. Luckily the ambulance crew got to him in time and thankfully he quickly made a full recovery. Gary is one of the nicest and most professional players I have been lucky enough to know and to this day I hold him in the highest esteem. To overcome type one diabetes and play at the top level for as long as he did is truly amazing and shows the character of the man. He is a great ambassador for Tottenham, Diabetes UK and mankind. A true legend.

To be a successful physio I believe you have to be on call 24 hours a day, seven days a week, and my players always knew they could call me any time of the day or night. During the 1992/93 season I had just returned home from a busy day at work at the training ground and was sitting down with my family to eat my dinner when the phone rang. It was a young Nick Barmby, who said he was with a youth team-mate who was complaining of feeling unwell. Nick said, 'We had a reserve game at White Hart Lane this afternoon and since then he feels dizzy and is tender on his left ribcage.' For some reason I had a feeling something wasn't right, so I explained to Nick how to take the player's radial pulse and count it. Nick tried to take it but just said, 'John, it is very fast and he is also very confused.' I needed to speak to the player so I asked Nick to put him on the phone, and I asked how he was. He responded, 'I am okay, John. I will have a good sleep tonight and see you in the morning.' My mind went into overdrive as I sensed something was seriously wrong. 'What happened in the game, did you get injured?' I asked. He said he hadn't, so I asked if he was sure. He confirmed that he had taken a 'whack in the ribs' during an aerial challenge, and that the area was 'a bit sore'. All those years ago while in a St John Ambulance competition in Cambridge I had to diagnose a patient with a ruptured spleen; the symptoms sounded the same. Could this be it? Am I panicking? Don't be silly, I said to myself, but my mind was made up. 'Nick, take him to Chase Farm Hospital immediately, I will leave now and meet you there.' So not for the first time dinner was left half-eaten as I rushed out of the door.

I arrived at the hospital to be met by a worried Nick as the player was being prepared for surgery. I went to see the consultant who told me, 'He has a ruptured spleen and it is critical that he is operated on immediately.' Nick phoned the player's family to tell them what was happening while I stayed by his bedside reassuring him everything would be okay. The operation was a success and he made a full recovery, minus one damaged spleen. When the surgeon came to see myself and Nick after the operation, he said to me, 'How on earth did you diagnose that over the phone?' I explained to him that I was once a lay instructor in first aid, so he then went on to say, 'Well done. If we hadn't operated on him when we did, he would have died in his sleep.' I owe the decision I made that day to a feeling I have developed over the years but I am so thankful for Nick's quick thinking. After an eventful night I arrived home at 5am and then was back up to Mill Hill at 9am with bloodshot eyes ready to treat the players before training. I look back all these years later and think of the time we won the winner of winners first aid tournament. I had to diagnose a ruptured spleen for the competition and was so relieved when I managed to do it for real to help save this young player's life.

Most people of my generation will remember the American world-class middle-distance runner Mary Decker. Immediately you think back to the 3,000m race at the Los Angeles Olympics in 1984 when she collided with the barefooted Zola Budd, which left Decker distraught and unable to continue. South

African Budd (who was representing Great Britain) was then booed by the home crowd as she finished seventh. Many people do not know that Decker's career was in major doubt in the mid-1970s due to persistent lower leg pain which resulted in weeks in plaster and understandably a loss of form. Her luck would change when she met the Dutch-born New Zealand middle-distance runner Dick Quax, who had suffered a similar injury. For several years he battled to overcome the pain in his legs and it wasn't until a revolutionary operation in the USA in 1975 that the issue was cured and he was able to train and race injury-free. Decker immediately underwent the same operation and a couple of weeks into her rehabilitation she started moving very carefully on grass, then to her amazement the pain she had suffered for years had gone.

The reason for mentioning Mary's story is that back in the 1970s and '80s the diagnosis of shin splints was bandied around to explain any lower-leg problems. However, with the improved knowledge and expertise we now know that a comprehensive examination is required to differentiate between certain lower-leg conditions such as medial tibial stress syndrome, stress fractures, compartmental syndrome and many more. MRI scans, bone scans and other tests are now used to give you the correct diagnosis, which then allows you choose the most suitable treatment with the utmost confidence. In the early '90s, our young striker Nick Barmby was having persistent bouts of pain and cramp in the lower leg, which were becoming extremely disabling. With the improved understanding and equipment that I have just mentioned, Nick was quickly diagnosed correctly and underwent two operations to cure the issue. After a short spell of rehabilitation he went on to have a great club and international career. If Nick had this injury

30 years earlier his career would most probably have been over before it began, so a big thank you must go to the likes of Dick Quax and Mary Decker, whose bravery and determination to overcome their injuries certainly paved the way for many more people to enjoy a career at the highest level.

If I could pass on one pearl of wisdom to any aspiring physiotherapists out there, it would be that even though you are working in a sports environment never assume the injury you are assessing is related to that particular sport. I remember some examples of this helped save the lives of a couple of my patients. One day I received a phone call from a local footballer who told me he was suffering from discomfort in his right knee. After examining him I found there was a small amount of discomfort in his patella, and something didn't seem right so I advised him to go to his doctor for further examination. This player came back to see me a week later and said the doctor told him there wasn't a problem and I was a clown for referring him. Undeterred, my sixth sense told me there was an underlying issue so I told him to immediately go to the hospital for an x-ray. Thankfully he took my advice as the x-ray discovered he had a bone tumour. Luckily, as it was diagnosed early it was treatable and I was pleased to discover he made a full recovery and went on to enjoy a long and successful career in the army.

The second occasion that sticks in my mind was when I received a call from a mother who told me her son had been injured playing football the previous day. Even though I had a fully booked clinic, something told me I needed to see him so I told her to bring him after my last appointment. That evening the doorbell rang and there stood the mother and her 14-year-old son, who was looking particularly poorly. He managed to get on the treatment bench and I asked him how it happened.

He told me he felt pain in his right knee after being tackled. As his mother helped him take off his tracksuit bottoms, I noticed he winced as the bottoms got caught on his ankle, which raised my concerns as he told me the initial pain was in his knee. Upon examination, the knee revealed tenderness to the touch but also heat radiated from the joint; the ankle also showed quite marked tenderness. Due to his appearance and lethargy I decided to take his temperature which was 40 degrees. Alarm bells sounded in my head and I told the mother to take him to A&E immediately, where the staff diagnosed an infectious viral condition that had caused septicaemia. He was admitted straight away and placed in the intensive care unit, and after a long stay in hospital I was thankful he made a full recovery. A few months later the pair of them visited my house and gave me a bottle of wine. I was so pleased to see them and the mother said, 'Thank you, John, for saving his life. The hospital told me that if he hadn't been seen that night, he would have most probably died.' After they had gone, I said a prayer of thanks that I had taken the time to see him after my clinic had finished.

When I moved into professional football, I soon noticed that I wasn't as quick as most of the other physios. So to help me get to the player a little bit quicker I would constantly scan the pitch and as soon as somebody had gone down, I would be off and approaching them even before the referee had called me on. Most referees of this era, such as Brian Hill and Clive Thomas, were okay with this and understood why I did it. However, I did notice that as the years passed the modern referees were sticklers for the rules and I would be constantly getting bollockings for running on before they had blown their whistle. I would never take the mickey but if I suspected a serious injury, I would be straight on no matter what. You get to know your players and how they reacted to an injury. Lads such as Mal Donaghy would never go down unless they were genuinely injured and I would have no hesitation in going on before I was called on even though that often meant facing the referee's wrath.

That said, running on to the pitch wasn't one of my strengths as a physio. There would sometimes be an occasion when a player from both teams went down at the same time and the crowd would love to see a physio race. I would try and get a head start but would often be overtaken at the last minute. I remember when Luton took on Middlesbrough and this happened between myself and Jimmy Headridge, who started running on at the same time. Jimmy was a great man and instead of running off into the distance he ran at the same pace alongside me so we would get to our players at the same time. The mutual respect we had for each other meant he wasn't going to show me up even though he had a fair turn of pace.

Upon reflection I honestly don't think I would survive in the modern game; I watch these super-fit physios run on to the pitch and realise my fitness would continually be in question. I was extremely lucky all those years ago that a young Luton manager had the guts to give me a chance and I just slotted into that era of football. My thirst for knowledge and love of the game carried me through to the top level. Along the way I was lucky enough to work with some great football people. I am proud of the trusting relationships I built with my players and due to this they always protected me and the majority are still good friends to this day.

* * *

Ricky Hill – Luton Town 1976–89

On 26 December 1987 I suffered a broken leg and badly damaged ankle ligaments in a challenge. This led to the expected long absence from being able to compete in training or games. During this period my club, Luton Town, continued to enjoy a wonderful season particularly in the cup competitions. This was born out in their progression to the Full Members' Cup Final against Reading at Wembley, to be followed by an FA Cup semi-final against Wimbledon, and lastly the League Cup Final at Wembley against the mighty Arsenal. These matches were due to span a one-month period from the end of March through to the end of April 1988.

Having received my injury just before the turn of the year I was really up against time in being able to participate in any of those games. While my broken leg had healed well, I was having issues with the fluid build-up around my ankle, which would swell up after any attempted exertion. This issue was ongoing and becoming particularly frustrating for me as I had been at the club for over 13 years and was desperate to play a part in this historic season. The physio at the time at Luton was someone who believed in the remedial side of the treatment of injuries and was not so much a hands-on type physio. This was a problem for me as despite the compression machine, ultrasound, and laser treatments the fluid was still evident. In my desperation to be involved in the upcoming games I decided to look for outside assistance in the treatment of my ankle.

When this awakening occurred, there was only one person who I sought to provide that assistance. John had been at Tottenham in recent times but had always maintained his long-standing private consultation and medical practice, which I had visited on numerous occasions. John and I go way back from his time as the head physiotherapist and head of all things medically related at Luton Town. John had treated me for several injuries, which was a common factor in a physical contact sport, and had been brilliant in his expertise, caring manner and empathetic support he always gave to all players who were under his care.

I called John to express my concerns relating to my current injury and desperation to do everything possible to have a chance to play some form of role in the forthcoming games. As always, John, without hesitation, said, 'Of course, Ricky, pop around when you get the opportunity, and I'll take a look for you.' Immediately I felt reinvigorated, and despite that sentence just being of a few words, the manner in which it was said gave me fresh hope that things may be all right. I visited John, who immediately diagnosed the problem and set about aiding its recovery. I was getting very little friction administered into the damaged area, which in turn would help with the blood supply required to assist with the healing at the club, but John did exactly the opposite, ensuring that the injury was not only receiving the assistance of the machines available but also that 'friction' in order to free up certain adhesions that were in and around the injury, and had been for months. I would visit John twice a week during the evening and my optimism increased with every meet.

I unfortunately missed the first two significant matches against Reading and Wimbledon and sat through them desperately wishing I was out there with the team, but could only sit and suffer as we lost out on both occasions. I was improving daily and I had managed to re-join the first team for training sessions roughly ten days before the League Cup Final. I would have to have a heavily strapped ankle in order to take part, but was prepared to do whatever was necessary to declare my availability for the final.

I visited John for the final time on the Wednesday before the Sunday's final. I was still unsure whether I would be able to put myself forward for selection, but John reassured me that the injury was strong and stable. I thanked John for all of his efforts and asked him how much was outstanding for his time and efforts in terms of payment. To my surprise, John just said, 'Don't be silly, Ricky, it is my pleasure.' That kind gesture epitomises exactly who John is in regards to always putting everyone first, never considering his own needs, and being totally committed to help if he could possibly do so. I did manage to be involved and was able to play my first competitive match in five months in the victory against Arsenal in a thrilling game. As the club's longest-serving player at the time, I felt immense pride in being part of a squad that brought the club's first and so far only major domestic cup victory. I can also say that without John's expertise, friendship, care and attention I would not now be the recipient of a winner's medal from a Wembley cup final. Thank you, John, for everything you have always done and more.

17

Other Memories

I HAVE come a long way since the day my son Andy followed me on to the pitch on that cold winter's afternoon at Tring Town, but this isn't the only funny memory I have while getting ready to treat a player.

Within the physio fraternity there is an unwritten rule that if two players on the same team go down injured at the same time then the opposing physio will go on to treat one of them. However, on one particular occasion on a wet and windy day at Old Trafford my counterpart seemed to forget this rule when two of my players went down at the same time but at opposite ends of the pitch. So after treating the first player I was amazed to see the other one still laying prone in the other penalty area. There was nothing else for it other than to limp across the entire pitch to the sound of booing and cat-calls from the partisan crowd. After finishing treating the second player, I was still breathing out of my arse as I walked behind the goal in front of the famous Stretford End. The whistles were still ringing in my ears but by this time in my career I had become hardened to it so I gave them a little bow and pretended to doff my cap. To my amazement they started cheering and next time I had to run on to the pitch they actually gave me a standing ovation! Years later I had a chat with Sir Bobby Robson and he said, 'I remember that day when you ran on at Old Trafford and what you did was great. It warmed my heart.' This meant so much to me coming from such a great man.

But it wasn't just Sir Bobby I was in awe of. There was an incident in the late 1980s at Tottenham with the charismatic Brian Clough. The White Hart Lane dugouts at that time had incredibly low roofs. I had discovered this to my cost on numerous occasions when in my haste I would whack my head as I raced off my seat to get on to an injured player. It didn't take me long to learn my lesson, so in an attempt to stop knocking myself out I decided I would stand in the tunnel instead of taking my place in the dugout. During a typical entertaining game between two footballing teams, Nottingham Forest were on the attack when all of a sudden, I heard a loud bang. As I looked to my left, I saw Cloughie holding his head as he had just succumbed to the low roof. He turned to me and said, 'Trainer, sort this f*****g roof out will you.' I replied, 'Sorry, Mr Clough, it is nothing to do with me.' He followed up with, 'Well it is now, trainer,' and with that he gave me a wink and returned to his seat. In my opinion, along with David Pleat, Brian was one of the best managers England never had. In his prime he was an inspirational manager and is someone I would definitely have loved to work for.

To have a successful football club I believe a vital ingredient is a very tight-knit group of players and staff who trust each other. However, just as in real life sometimes people can wander off the straight and narrow and do things they wouldn't normally do. This happened at Luton Town in the early 1980s. While the players went training or played in a game, I would be responsible for looking after their precious valuables. Every day I would put a bag in the dressing room and the players would place all of the items that they wanted to keep safe in it. I would then guard it with my life; wherever I went the valuables came with me, even as I ran on to the pitch during a game.

Unfortunately there was a short spell at the club when small amounts of money would go missing out of the players' pockets as their clothes hung on the pegs in the first team dressing room. One morning the players had gone out to train, and I had finished treating the injuries so popped out to watch the lads. After a short while I decided to go back into the treatment room and as I opened the door to the dressing room, I caught one of the apprentices with his hand in one of the players' jacket pockets. I had caught him red-handed and the mystery of the missing money was over. As soon as he saw me the young lad burst into tears, pleading with me not to tell the manager as he would immediately be sacked in disgrace and his budding football career over before it began. Deep down I knew he was a good lad; he had gone through a difficult upbringing and football seemed to give him some sort of structure and belonging in his life. I asked him, 'Why are you stealing from your team-mates?' He replied, 'John, I am really sorry, I didn't know what else to do, it's not an excuse but I have been gambling and owe money.' While I decided what to do, I told him to put all the money he had taken back into the players' pockets.

To risk his career, he must have been at a real low point in his life. I thought if I reported him to the manager then his life would only go in a downward spiral, so I decided to give him a second chance. We sat down and had a heart to heart chat and I said, 'I won't report you, but if you step out of line once more, I will have no choice but to tell the manager. If that happens then it won't just be you being sacked but I will also be in deep trouble, so don't let me down.' He agreed and to his credit, he was as good as his word and stayed out of trouble. Over the next few years he worked extremely hard and earned a contract as a professional footballer but never really made it at the top level. Ironically, many years later I was working at my private practice when my next patient walked through the door. I immediately recognised him; he had grown into a well-mannered human being and had become a successful businessman. We started talking about his time at Luton and he said, 'Thank you John, for trusting me all of those years ago. I would never have let you down.' That decision could have backfired on us both, but he had turned his life around and I felt pleased that I made the right choice.

Sometimes people are beyond help and are too far down the road of criminality. As with most clubs during that time, Luton were always on the hunt for a hidden gem of a player who wouldn't cost much money. One summer the coaching staff had invited a couple of players to stay over for a two-day trial. On the first day I wandered across to watch the trialists play in a friendly game but it was clear to see that one of them was out of his depth and had no chance of earning a professional contract. Undeterred, the lads turned up the next day, and shortly after training started both of the trialists came to see me in the treatment room. One of them said to me that he wasn't feeling very well, so as I examined him the other went off to return to training (or so I thought!). I couldn't find anything wrong with him and told him to return to his digs and I would get the doctor to call him when he came in at lunchtime. As soon as Dr Berry came to the ground, I asked him to call the trialist to see if he was okay, but despite constant attempts there was no answer. I was getting a bit concerned until the coaching staff came in and said, 'Somebody has been in our changing room and nicked all of our valuables.' The penny dropped as there was no sign of either trialist. They had come back early with the intention of stealing as much as they could and while one distracted me the other helped themselves before the pair made a sharp exit. We later discovered they had been caught but not before targeting numerous other unsuspecting football clubs.

Being a physio in professional football occasionally gave me the chance to treat some of my old heroes. I would listen intently as they told me stories of the great games, players and managers from their past. I heard tales about the legendary Spurs side managed by Bill Nicholson and including players such as Danny Blanchflower, Johnny White, Tommy Harper, Jimmy Greaves and Dave Mackay to name but a few. Over the years I have treated quite a few old Luton players who I had the privilege to watch as I was growing up. But it wasn't just the Luton players I remember watching; I was also lucky enough to watch players of the calibre of Duncan Edwards and the rest of the Busby Babes, the majestic John Charles, Sir Stanley Matthews and Denis Law.

A real highlight for me was when I had the honour to meet the great Stan Mortensen at a Football Writers' Association dinner. I went over to his table to get his autograph and amazingly he asked me to sit down for a chat. He relived the great 1953 FA Cup Final between Blackpool and Bolton, which became famously known as the Matthews Final. Stan scored a hat-trick and I listened in awe as he relived every moment and brought that game to life for me.

One of my favourite players of all time was the legendary Bobby Moore. I never got to meet him properly but would sometimes say hello as he was a regular fixture in the press box at White Hart Lane, even when he was extremely ill. I can honestly say I shed a few tears when he died. I remember saying to Terry Venables that it was wrong that one of our greatest players, our World Cup-winning captain, was not looked after by the FA and I couldn't believe he didn't receive the knighthood he so richly deserved.

In my first spell at Luton I was lucky enough to look after some players who have gone on to become club legends, such as David Moss, Paul Walsh, Brian Stein, Mick Harford, Steve Foster and of course the brilliant Ricky Hill. In my opinion Ricky was harshly treated by England and I am in no doubt that he should have won many more caps and been a regular for his country. All of the players meant a lot to me and I wonder what they would cost in today's transfer market.

Another player from that squad who I have fond memories of is Wayne Turner. Sometimes you meet somebody in your life who you form an immediate and lifelong bond with and Wayne is one of those people. I first met him when he was a second-year pro at the club in the early 1980s and was delighted to see him progress into a first-team regular. Even though our football careers took us to different clubs we always kept in touch and after we had both retired from the game, there would always be a knock on my door on Christmas Eve and it would be Wayne with a big smile and a bottle of wine. One particular year Wayne popped in to see me and I had been struggling with a leak in my conservatory roof. Somehow I had managed to scramble up there to try and temporarily repair it until after the holiday period. Unfortunately, the repair didn't work and when Wayne found out he said, 'Don't worry, Shez, I will sort it out for you.' I tried to stop him but he quickly climbed the ladders in the pouring rain and in his best clothes. That showed the calibre of the man and nothing was too much trouble for him; he is a real gentleman.

At Tottenham I was lucky enough to see the silky skills of Glenn Hoddle and Chris Waddle. They are two players I definitely would have paid to watch; the hairs on the back of your neck would stand up as you watched the teasing runs of Waddle down the White Hart Lane wing. We also had other world-class players such as Ossie Ardiles, Ray Clemence, Richard Gough, Chris Hughton and of course our dependable captain Gary Mabbutt. All of them great footballers but more importantly great men as well. After David Pleat left, the squad changed and in came some more fantastic players such as goalkeeper Erik Thorstvedt, Justin Edinburgh, Nayim, Gary Lineker and the most gifted player I ever had the pleasure looking after, Paul Gascoigne. I could go on with naming great players and I have to pinch myself now to realise I had the undoubted privilege to look after these footballing icons and watch them display their skills and dedication at stadiums both here and abroad.

It wasn't just famous footballers I had the pleasure to look after at Spurs. One of the most funny and surreal moments during my time there was when I found myself treating a local racing greyhound. I had recently been introduced to the father of one of our apprentices. This man was a well-known greyhound trainer and was a dead ringer for Chas Hodges out of Chas & Dave. This particular morning, he had just dropped off his son to training when he wandered over to the treatment room to see me. I popped outside to see what he wanted and to my amazement he said, 'John, I need your help. Can you give one of my greyhounds some ultrasound please?' I explained to him that although I was a dog lover, if Terry came in to see a greyhound on the bench next to one of his star international players then I would get the sack! However, he wasn't going to give in that easily and went on to say, 'But he is one of my best dogs and is due to run at White City in a couple of days. If you can get him fit, he has a great chance of winning and as a thank you I will put a score on the nose for you [£20 to win].' I thought what harm could it do and a few quid on a dog sounded appealing, so I came up with a plan and said, 'Okay, but you will need to come in early tomorrow. The only way we can do it without Terry finding out is if you hold him [the greyhound] outside and stick his arse through the side window and I will give him a quick go on the ultrasound, but if anyone comes in you will have to make a hasty retreat.' That night I did a bit of research on dogs and the next morning my plan worked a treat. Luckily nobody found out about our unusual patient and the ultrasound must have made a difference to our four-legged friend as he stormed home in first place the following evening.

This wasn't the last time I would turn my hand to impersonating Dr Dolittle as after retiring from football I would sometimes be asked to treat the odd greyhound at my clinic. By that stage I had discovered that acupuncture worked well on the dogs. However, I dread to think what my next patient in the waiting room would be thinking as when the needles went in, loud howling could be heard from the other side of the door!

Luton are well known as being one of the first clubs to invest in an artificial pitch. However, I remember the first professional game to be played on such a surface in Europe, on 1 September 1981 at Loftus Road between Queens Park Rangers and Luton. The enterprising QPR board, led by chairman Jim Gregory, laid the pitch in 1981 and over the next two years it helped them reach the FA Cup Final and win the Second Division title. The two managers that day were the talented Terry Venables at QPR and the young, knowledgeable, up-and-coming David Pleat at Luton. We travelled to London on the morning of the game for a training session to get to know the new pitch and also for the players to test their footwear. It had all the makings to be an entertaining game between two teams who tried to play football the right way. The hosts opened the scoring in the 34th minute when Andy King netted from a Bob Hazel cross but we grew into the game and started to get used to the pitch, resulting in us equalising through Mark Aizlewood who lobbed the onrushing QPR keeper John Burridge. Ricky Hill got the winner with a stunning drive in the 84th minute after Steve White won the ball from Gerry Francis.

Luton laid an artificial pitch in 1985. It was officially called Omniturf and was filled with sand. I have no doubt that this type of surface helped hone the players' technical skill but to what cost? I was always concerned about the impact on the players' joints due to the constant jarring and also the horrific burns they would receive after a sliding tackle. I actually wrote a report at the end of that first season for the club, highlighting the effects it was having on the players, but it mysteriously disappeared. The FA actually confirmed the banning of artificial pitches at elite level in 1988. From 2014 and due to increased technology 3G pitches were allowed to be used in all rounds of the FA Cup and the following season National League teams could use them for league games. The pristine grass pitches of today have made a difference to the quality of modern football but looking back, the muddy, boggy pitches of yesteryear added a lot to the game I love.

A funny memory regarding Luton's plastic pitch was from my first visit back after leaving to go to Spurs. After laying all the medical kit out in the away team dressing room, I had time to spare so I wandered down the tunnel for a breath of fresh air. As I got on to the pitch the Luton groundsman Charlie Garner, who had recently been appointed, was carrying out his final preparations before the game. I asked Charlie how he was doing and he replied, 'Fine, thank you. Are you the referee?' I couldn't resist winding him up, so I said, 'Yes, how's the pitch?' He added, 'I am just finishing the preparation and re-marking any lines that have faded,' to which I said, 'Before you finish the marking, could you give it a final cut please, I understand you have a special mower to cut the plastic and the grass appears to be too long.' By now Charlie had fallen for the wind-up and said, 'Are you joking? This is a plastic pitch.' The discussion went on for a while and just before he attempted to throttle me, the Luton goalkeeper Les Sealey strolled down the tunnel and said, 'Hello John, how are you?' 'Fine thank you, Les,' I said. Charlie interrupted and asked Les, 'Do you know him?' 'Yes, that's John, the physio,' came his response. Instead of throttling me, Charlie just started to laugh and said a few choice words!

Not all of my memories of Luton were as entertaining as winding up the groundsman. In my mind for all the wrong reasons is the infamous FA Cup quarter-final on 13 March 1985 between Luton and Millwall. I arrived at the ground at my usual time to start the pre-match preparations and to also treat a couple of players. While travelling in, I heard on the radio that there had been trouble in the town centre and the Arndale Shopping Centre was forced to close early to avoid further damage to the shops. After completing my prep I liked to wander down the tunnel to get some fresh air before the rest of the squad started to arrive. As I stood by the side of the pitch, there seemed a peculiar atmosphere in the ground even though there were only a few people milling around. Unfortunately nobody could anticipate the carnage that was about to be unleashed at Kenilworth Road in the next few hours.

I returned to the treatment room and started to prepare the players for the game. Some of the lads headed out for the warm-up but I realised something was wrong when they quickly returned to the dressing room. They seemed to sense trouble in the air and instead of the usual banter and positive atmosphere there was a feeling of dread about what the next few hours were going to bring. As we walked out for the start of the game, I vividly remember seeing a packed – in truth, it was overflowing – stadium. The referee David Hutchinson got the game under way, but after 14 minutes the rioting away supporters started climbing over the metal railings and on to the side of the pitch, so he was forced to stop the game. The players and staff then went back into the dressing rooms for their own safety.

Twenty-five minutes later the game restarted but only after Millwall manager George Graham had pleaded with the away supporters to behave and stay in the stands. The fear of the fans fighting and encroaching back on to the pitch was never far away. Somehow, we managed to get to half-time 1-0 in front after Brian Stein had broken down the right-hand side and scored with a great shot that went in after clipping the bottom of the post. During the break David Pleat spoke to the referee, who promised he would somehow try to finish the game; I admire the way he handled such a difficult situation and I dread to think what would have happened if he had abandoned the match at that point. The feeling in the dressing room was shock at what had happened over the past 70 minutes.

Shock then turned to concern for our families as we realised no part of the ground was safe. Therefore, many of the staff and players managed to get a message to our loved ones to go home immediately.

We went out for the second half with trepidation, especially Les Sealey, who had to defend the goal that was the furthest away from the tunnel and in front of the away fans. Les was bombarded with missiles including a knife and snooker balls, and I had never seen him stand so far away from his goal. As full time approached we were getting surrounded in the dugouts so I told our substitute David Moss to warm up and not to come back. The referee also told Les that he would give him a signal just before he was about to blow the final whistle so he could run like the clappers and get to safety.

When the whistle went both sets of players sprinted towards the tunnel, but the fans weren't far behind. As the coaching staff left the dugout I was grabbed by one of the thugs, and there was no way I was going to get involved in any fighting so with all the force I could muster I swivelled round and hit him with my medical bag. This seemed to do the trick and luckily he let go, so I then ran as fast as I could to get to safety. Without doubt it was utter carnage and the trouble after the game was by far the worst violence of the night. The so-called Millwall supporters began to fight the police and threw seats and anything else they could rip up. Our poor old groundsman Dick Wassell wasn't as quick as everyone else and he found himself locked out of the tunnel, but the double doors were soon unlocked and he was dragged to safety.

I had never seen anything quite like it in all of my time in football. What happened that night raised a lot of questions. Why wasn't it an all-ticket game? Why weren't there enough police and stewards? As the violence erupted, they were outnumbered and completely unprepared. The scenes that night damaged our national game, and the following day England lost out to West Germany for the right to host the 1988 European Championship despite being favourites. Was that game partly to blame? Nobody will ever know but whenever I look back on that fateful night I break out into a cold sweat. The entire experience was distressing, brutal and harrowing and as a result of this game, Luton chairman David Evans banned away supporters and introduced identity cards.

* * *

Wayne Turner – Luton Town 1978–85

A genuine guy, honest man and a brilliant physio. That's how I would describe John. A man's man, with a real caring streak. Those qualities made him a vital part of the Luton Town backroom staff in the late 1970s and most of the '80s.

I first met John at the tender age of 18, when I was a second-year pro and he joined the club as the full-time physio. His pipe-puffing, calm persona quickly won the lads over. Not only was he very knowledgeable, but he also insisted on the latest machinery to go with that talent. One in particular stands out for me, the diapulse machine. I believe only us and Manchester United had it at the time. The lads called it R2/D2 as it looked like a robot.

When I went to Lincoln City on loan in 1981, I got my big toe stamped on while playing away against Reading on the Saturday, so on the Sunday I was in for treatment at Lincoln. I drove two hours up the motorway to then be given a one-metre length of hosepipe. I was then instructed to attach the hose to the cold tap and run it on my big toe for 20 minutes. Where was John and the 'robot'?! I argued my case and was allowed to continue my treatment at my parent club, in the safe and caring hands of John. As I mentioned earlier, John was miles ahead with his knowledge and his insistence on the latest technology. This example just confirmed that.

While John was an outstanding physio, he was also a wonderful listener. When you were injured, all your other problems got magnified and you would pour all your anxieties out to him. He would stay calm, logical and give you the reassurance you required and most importantly it would stay private between you two.

I used to love our Sunday-morning gatherings. After the game a group of about six of us young lads used to hit the town for our beloved Saturday night out, releasing all the pressure that had built up in the previous week (especially if we didn't have a midweek game coming up). Treatment would be at 9am, and we would all roll in one by one for a catch-up of the previous night's events. Some of us were in the same clothes we had gone out in, and others with pieces of clothing totally missing. If you did have an injury you would get treatment from John; if not you would jump in the big communal bath and relax the morning away. On the treatment table or in the bath the sound of laughter would ring out as we recited the stories of the night before. There was not a better feeling in the world than a night out after winning a high-pressured football match hours before.

John's physio room was such a happy place, which is strange when you think that it was a situation where you were normally in if you were injured. He made it such a positive environment. Serious rehab, but with a smile on your face. John's wit and sense of humour was lethal, accompanied with an infectious laugh.

We worked together until I moved to Coventry in 1985, and even then, for the rest of my career I would pop to his house to seek a second opinion on any injury I had picked up.

For over 40 years John has been a trusted and loyal friend. Until he recently moved away, John and Betty welcomed me over ever Christmas Eve for a drink as far back as I can remember. Though I would have seen him throughout the year, it was a morning set it stone, that we both enjoyed. Always having a laugh, reciting stories while getting ready for the big day.

Wonderful times, and treasured memories.

John (Shezza) was and still is a true gent.

18

Fun on the Fairway

WHEN I moved to Whitbread in 1974, I discovered a sport that I still enjoy and play to this day. Golf is not only a great game but it has also allowed me to meet so many fantastic people who have become lifelong friends. To help me settle in at my new job all those years ago I joined the Whitbread golf society, which had regular golf days at different courses around the county. I had never played before so I soon found myself at the local course with a set of second-hand clubs and somehow, I managed to hack my way round and from that day I was hooked. Quite a few lessons later I was ready to take on the world with a handicap of 28 and over the next four or five years I continued to play, but regrettably my handicap didn't get much lower and when I joined Luton Town in 1979, golf was unfortunately put on the back-burner.

The nature of my new job in professional football meant that any spare time was at a premium and my golf clubs were pushed to the back of the shed to gather dust. Sometimes I had the opportunity to blow off the cobwebs and get the clubs back out, as I did at Ricky Hill's testimonial golf day at Beadlow Manor. On the morning of Ricky's special day, I had to go to Kenilworth Road to treat the injured players. It was a particularly busy morning and before I knew it the tee-off time was fast approaching so I travelled straight to the course and just in the nick of time I limped on to the first tee to be met with looks of disappointment from my playing companions, as I was still wearing my work clothes including the bright orange jacket I wore on matchdays.

After introducing ourselves, I was horrified to discover that the four-ball was made up of myself, two professionals and one scratch golfer. I can imagine that my fellow competitors had paid a lot of money to play in Ricky's golf day and I don't think they were too pleased to be forced to spend the afternoon with a 28-handicapper dressed in a tracksuit. Things didn't go too well for the next few hours as most of the time was spent looking for my ball and after one of the worst rounds of my life, I vowed to throw the clubs in the bin.

After enjoying a couple of drinks to celebrate the day it was then time for the prize-giving to start. I knew that our team had no chance of picking up an award so you can imagine my amazement when my name was read out, 'The prize for the worst dressed golfer goes to the one and only John Sheridan.' I then had to take the walk of shame up to the front of the clubhouse to collect this special prize and for the next few weeks, my golfing attire was a topic for plenty of mickey-taking in the treatment room.

A few years before Ricky's testimonial, David Pleat had arranged a short trip to the Isle of Wight to play a couple of friendlies and raise some much-needed funds for the club. As soon as we arrived, some of the lads were delighted to discover that the hotel we were staying at had a nine-hole golf course attached to it. After breakfast the next day a few of us headed off for a game, and my group included the Welsh international defender Paul Price. Back then I smoked a pipe and while standing on the tee of a difficult par three with the green surrounded by bunkers, Paul said to me, 'John, I will give you a million to one you can't get the ball on the green by using your pipe as a tee and hitting the ball with a driver.' I've always wanted to be a millionaire so I took the bet and got my pound out. Somehow, I managed to get the ball balanced on the pipe and then out came my trusty old driver while the rest of the group waited in anticipation. Amazingly, I managed to hit one of the best shots of my life and the ball landed on the green and came to a stop three feet from the pin. Paul fell to the floor in amazement and said, 'How on earth did you do that, it's not possible.' To this day he never paid up to make me an instant millionaire or even paid for my pipe, which was scattered in pieces on the tee box never to be smoked again!

When I left Luton to go to Tottenham in 1986 I was pleased to discover a lot of the lads were keen golfers and had low handicaps. The players of that era enjoyed a lot of free time during the week and it was a regular occurrence that after training had finished, they would head off to the nearest course for a round. The role of a physio meant that you would often have to stay in the afternoon to continue with the treatment and rehab of the long-term injured players. But if the workload allowed, I managed to get the odd game and sometimes if they were short, I would get a call-up to an invitation day to represent the club.

Trips abroad usually allowed more opportunities to play as I had a bit more free time, such as in the summer of 1987 when the club travelled to Bermuda for an end-of-season break. A highly regarded local golf course had kindly invited the Tottenham players and staff to play, so we arrived at this beautiful seaside course with views of the sparkling North

Atlantic Ocean. I was lucky enough to be in a four-ball with Glenn Hoddle, Ossie Ardiles and Ray Clemence, who was my partner. You can only dream of playing golf with legends like these men and all these years later I do have to pinch myself to think that it was really me.

Not to be left out of the fun, Mitchell Thomas came along with our group and acted as Glenn's chauffeur in the golf buggy. Unfortunately for Glenn, Mitchell wasn't the greatest driver and at one point Glenn was almost catapulted into the air as he hit a tree stump at full speed. Despite Mitchell's best efforts to injure Glenn we had a great time and enjoyed a close game, mainly due to Ray as he played out of his skin and carried me on his broad shoulders as I hacked my way round the course.

As we made our way on to the last tee, the game was all square and we had everything to play for. The 18th was a difficult par four with a dog-leg to the right. After I somehow got the ball to the corner of the dog-leg, the green and clubhouse suddenly came into view. What an intimidating sight; the green was surrounded by bunkers but worst of all the balcony of the clubhouse was full of members and Tottenham players eager to watch us. As usual I was the shortest off the tee, so I was first to play my approach. I stood over the ball and with trepidation I looked into the sky and said to myself, 'Lord, if I never hit another decent golf shot then please just let me hit the green this time.' I swung the club with everything I had and for one of the first times that day, to mine and everyone else's amazement I struck the ball cleanly and watched as it flew through the air heading towards the pin; it landed on the green and rolled to about four feet from the hole. The balcony erupted and Ray looked at me and said, 'Bloody hell John, where did that come from? Why couldn't you have hit the ball like that on the previous 17 holes?' I replied, 'I was saving the best until last, Ray. Over to you!'

The other three didn't get close to my ball and as I strolled up the fairway towards the green it felt as if I was about to win the Open Championship as I lapped up the applause. Even though I had played crap all day, it was all forgotten as the standing ovation got louder and louder the closer we got to the green. I even managed to hole the putt; what a great way to finish a truly memorable day. It was an absolute pleasure and honour to play with these lads and an occasion that I will never forget.

Another memorable round abroad was during a mid-season visit to Fort Lauderdale. My four-ball for the day at Coral Ridge Country Club comprised two club members and our record-breaking centre-forward Clive Allen. We enjoyed a good game on Florida's sunny south-eastern coast and as we returned to the clubhouse for a well-deserved beer, we were met by the club professional. She said to myself and Clive, 'I would like you to meet my dad,' and proudly introduced us to Julius Boros, who had won the US Open in 1952 and 1963, the PGA Championship in 1968, and numerous other competitions. Julius's game was the complete opposite to mine as he was known for his effortless-looking swing and he had a great record on difficult golf courses. It was a privilege to meet a golfing great and he was such a humble man even though he had achieved so much in the game.

After leaving full-time football I had many more opportunities to play golf. My hip replacement had been a godsend and it allowed me to play more competitively, so I decided to join South Beds Golf Club in Luton and a short while later I was lucky enough to be accepted as a member at the prestigious Woburn club. Over the years I have enjoyed many rounds of golf at some of the best courses around the world, but more importantly I have forged many lifetime friendships with some fantastic people such as Sam Hill, Peter Doyle, Bill Astbury, Barney Gill and Joe Ashmall.

One of my favourite places to play is Fancourt, which is situated in George on the western cape of South Africa. It had plenty of water and wildlife and truly some of the fastest greens I have ever played on. In Scotland the best course has to be Castle Stuart in Inverness which has infinity greens that seem to sparkle in the Moray Firth. In Ireland there are so many great courses but I loved Waterville in County Kerry, where again I played with my two sons. It overlooks the majestic Atlantic Ocean and the town boasts a statue of Charlie Chaplin. I believe he spent a lot of time there enjoying the Irish hospitality, which in my opinion is the best in the world.

At my peak I managed to get down to a respectable handicap of 14. I couldn't hit the ball too far but it was usually straight; that is how I have tried to live my life but I must say I have hit a few shanks along the way!

I was deeply honoured to be asked to become the Luton Irish Golf Society captain for 2010. Since joining the society ten years before I had developed a lifelong friendship with some of these lads and this was the icing on the cake. They referred to me as a 'Plastic Paddy' but in fact my dad's parents were from County Clare in the fair isles. Those of you who play golf know that to be a captain of a golf society for a year takes a lot of time, effort and support and I was lucky that my family were there to help. I couldn't have done it without my eldest son Andy, who spent a lot of time planning events and also sourcing the prizes. I will be forever grateful for his hard work and expertise, which made my captain's year so successful, but more importantly I am extremely proud of the support and love he has always shown me.

It was a great year and we enjoyed many fabulous tournaments, but the highlight was definitely Captain's Weekend. We travelled to Le-Touquet in France for a three-day jolly boys' outing, the format for which was a Ryder Cup-style competition of Europe v the Rest of the World, two teams of ten with different-coloured t-shirts for each day. The coach set off at 6am on a cold Friday from a pub car park in Luton and from what I remember some of the lads enjoyed a liquid breakfast. The t-shirts were handed out on the coach and immediately the banter started between the two teams.

However, I did drop an almighty clanger the next day. Although we were a close bunch of mates, there was a mix of Catholics and Protestants within the group. For those of you who know your religion, Catholics are associated with the colour green and Protestants are associated with orange, so you can imagine my horror when on Saturday lunchtime orange shirts were handed out to one of the teams. The Catholics in the group went mad but did me the honour of wearing them for the golf, although as soon as they had finished their rounds the shirts came off and went straight in the bin. We had a fantastic time with lots of laughs and made some great memories, but from what I remember the standard of golf deteriorated as the weekend went on.

A sombre but memorable part of the trip was during a planned visit to the Étaples Military Cemetery, just outside Boulogne. It has over 11,000 graves from victims of the two world wars. Everyone found the experience extremely emotional and it made us realise the sacrifices people made to allow us to live in peace.

Another trip I will always remember is travelling to the USA with my two sons Andy and Paul in 2005. After landing in Washington we enjoyed a road trip through Virginia, North and South Carolina, stopping off to play golf, sightseeing and generally enjoying ourselves, culminating in watching a day's play at the US Open at Pinehurst. Our hire car racked up a few thousand miles and it truly was a dad's dream to experience such a precious time with his two sons. Andy also had a spell in South Africa working as a robotics engineer. I flew out to visit him just before he returned to the UK. We had a brilliant time travelling the garden route and playing some fantastic courses while also enjoying some of the local delicacies.

I don't play as much as I would like to now, but whenever possible I love to take on my eldest grandson, Jake. He is extremely talented and aspires to be a professional golfer but I can still occasionally beat him if he gives me enough shots.

19

Looking Back

REFLECTING ON my career, I can honestly say it was a privilege to work for two great clubs. I was lucky enough to enjoy a fantastic relationship with both sets of fans, who always gave me great support for which I will forever be grateful. I have mentioned players in my book as it would not be my story without them. The injuries I have described have either been well documented in the media or if not, I have gained permission to include their names, so no ethical bridges have been crossed. Another reason for describing the injuries in such detail is to hopefully help any up-and-coming young physios.

A good physiotherapist is in a unique situation at a football club. He is the players' therapist, psychologist, confidant and can sometimes be an advisor. The treatment room is an inner sanctum for a footballer and what is said in there is always in the strictest confidence. I understand a physio also has a duty to the manager and this can sometimes lead to a conflict of interest but I genuinely believe that if a player can speak openly to you then it will benefit the entire club. In all my time in both non-league and professional football I can honestly say that I have never betrayed the confidence of a player and would always try and help them in any way possible. Sometimes if a player had an issue and felt unable to speak out, I would agree to be the go-between and say to the manager that it might be worth having a chat with that particular individual, then it was up to him if he wanted to open up and discuss his issue.

One of my biggest allies during my career was my daughter Debbie, who from the age of 15 wrote all of the medical records for the players. After leaving school she trained as a medical secretary and found she had a natural talent in this profession. Debbie quickly went on to be very successful, culminating in her becoming the practice manager for the acclaimed surgeon Jerry Gilmore in Harley Street. Despite all of her hard work and long hours, she would always return home and update my players' records in an immaculate fashion. This was such an important part of running a successful medical department at both Luton and Spurs; the detail and care she showed updating them helped immensely during player transfers and also importantly when I had to produce the records to the American surgeon Jim Andrews and Lazio staff during Paul Gascoigne's transfer. It left them in no doubt of the hard work that had been shown by Paul and the medical team at Spurs to return him to full fitness. Thank you, Debbie.

For over 50 years I have treated players for their injuries and general welfare, from the humble amateur on the local park to the best players in the world at some of the greatest venues. I can honestly say that I felt an immense sense of pride and satisfaction helping each and every one of them. From my early years in non-league football to working in the Football League, I have had the pleasure to work with a variety of managers, all with different ideas and characteristics. I always tried to build a good working relationship with them all. However, I will be eternally grateful to David Pleat for giving me a chance in professional football. He was brave to employ a physiotherapist with a disability but I still had to grab the opportunity with both hands. Throughout all the time I worked with David at Luton and Tottenham I always found him very easy to work with; he was extremely loyal to me and I will always have the utmost respect for him.

When Terry Venables took over from David at Tottenham in 1988, I honestly believed my days at this great club were numbered. My good friend Trevor Hartley had just been shown the door after David's exit and I was sure I would be next. To be fair to Terry he could have quite easily sacked me and brought in his own physio. But he is an astute man and I'm sure he had done his homework on me. Since joining Spurs the previous year, I had built up a good trusting relationship with the lads, who liked me and knew I would look after them. Terry knew he could trust me and I would always give him, the club and the players my total support and commitment. He always thought I was too soft with them but this was my way of dealing with them and over the years I have had hardly any problems at all. They knew I wouldn't run to the manager to get them fined; I was a great believer that if you had an issue then a man-to-man chat would usually resolve any problems.

Throughout my career, I truly believe the players didn't have an issue with my disability. Saying that, I knew Gazza would do a great impression of me bending down to treat an injured player. A few years ago I met David Seaman in the pro shop at Brocket Hall Golf Club, and when he realised who I was he said, 'Gazza used to do a great impression of you,' then recreated it. It was extremely funny but it was very surreal to see the great David Seaman doing an impression of me!

I count myself extremely lucky to have met some of football's greatest names and characters, and there are two people I would have loved to work for. The first is Sir Bobby Robson, a real gentleman and someone that I had the utmost respect for. The second is the popular ex-West Ham manager John Lyall. I had the pleasure of getting to know John extremely well during the short time he spent as a technical advisor at Spurs in 1989. We often enjoyed an early-morning cup of tea in the treatment room at the training ground, where he would reminisce about his time in football and would often pass on a few words of wisdom. Unfortunately both men are no longer with us and I am not ashamed to say that I shed a few tears when they passed away.

As well as becoming friends to these fantastic characters, I have also been fortunate to meet and treat some inspirational people who are not directly involved in football, such as world championship boxers Barry McGuigan and Billy Schwer, actor John Cleese and the legendary Luton Town director Eric Morecambe. However, one person in particular stands out – Isaiah Stein, the father of Brian and Mark. Isaiah was a political activist from South Africa who was instrumental in the fight against apartheid and was tortured for his beliefs. He would sometimes pop into the treatment room at Luton, a very humble man who clearly loved all of his children dearly. It was a real honour and pleasure to meet him.

Over the years the role of a physio has definitely changed. If I was starting out in my career today, I am not 100 per cent sure that I would still get the opportunities I enjoyed decades back. The physios in the modern game seem to be getting younger and quicker than ever. Back in the old days I remember watching the old Luton trainers such as Frank King and later Reg Game run on the pitch to treat injuries with their bucket and sponge. They both did a great job and had a wealth of experience which was an immense advantage, as many of the trainers and sponge men at that time were former pros who just wanted to stay involved in the game.

The opportunity to learn and develop has improved over the years. When I first started, the FA ran various regional medical courses culminating in the prestigious three-year treatment of injury course held at Lilleshall. This course was run by Paddy Armour and his excellent tutors. Paddy would put the fear of god into me but what a pioneer of sports medicine. One of the tutors I remember from that time was Jimmy Headridge, who passed away much too early doing the job he loved at Manchester United in 1982.

The support for physios has continually improved. Medical societies were being formed to help improve sports treatment from grassroots to the highest level. I would often attend the FA regional meetings in the south-east where eminent lecturers such as Dr John Crane (Arsenal) and Dr Vernon Edwards (England and Watford) gave their time and knowledge. These meetings also gave you an opportunity to meet your fellow therapists, who would always offer their help and advice. The Society of Sports Therapists, which was set up in 1990, has been a continual support for physiotherapists up and down the country since its inception. The chairman Professor Graham Smith has worked tirelessly to nurture this society through many stages of development. I am proud to say I was an original member of this organisation and in fact made an honorary life member for services to football, which was a proud moment.

The number of medical staff employed at football clubs at the top level today has increased ten-fold. I look at sports medicine and realise the massive strides that have been made in my lifetime. Without doubt our country has become the home of experts in this field but looking back the pioneers in football shine out like a beacon of light. Surgeons such as Jerry Gilmore and David Dandy have played a major part in the advance of sports medicine but also saved many players' careers.

After five decades in football, I think back to what my role was when I first walked through the door of the Kenilworth Road treatment room in 1978. I quickly learnt you had to have a comprehensive knowledge of sports medicine and lifesaving skills that you could put into practice quickly and efficiently. Players had to trust you explicitly as you were often a confidant to them and their families. Sometimes you had to protect them from themselves and outside influences. All players wanted to play but occasionally you would have to make the unpopular decision to tell them they hadn't recovered fully or weren't fit enough. I would always put their welfare before football as players of that era would generally have to carry on working after they had retired from playing. You owed it to them to minimise any permanent damage to their bodies so they could live a good standard of life.

You had to be willing to work 24/7 and understand that days off would be few and far between. I remember after a good result David Pleat would sometimes say, 'You can have Monday off, lads. John, what time do you want the injured players in?'

It is like no other profession, job or vocation. A knowledge of nutrients, a bit of understanding of psychology, dedication, compassion and a love of looking after the health and welfare of your players; all of these things mixed together should make a half-decent physiotherapist.

You also need to have a smile on your face, help the manager, staff and of course the players which will in turn create a successful and happy football club but most importantly enjoy it all. I certainly have.

Postscript

Jake Findlay – Luton Town 1978–85

I remember John joining us in the 1979/80 season. We had had a couple of tough years but a lot of new players had been brought in by David Pleat and things were finally starting to gel. On John's first day the dressing room door popped open and in walked David Pleat, David Coates and another guy with a limp. David asked us to sit down and then said, 'Lads, as you know our previous physio Roy has left to become assistant at Arsenal, but I am pleased to say that this our new physio, John Sheridan.'

He was quiet at the start and probably in awe of entering the harsh world of professional football with his local side but we immediately noticed the difference in the quality of treatment. Usually you would go and see a physio and after a bit of heat he would say, 'You're okay now, son, go back to training.' However, this wasn't the case with John, who would give you a proper examination, diagnose the problem and then tell you how it would be treated. All the lads thought, 'Wow, we have someone who genuinely cares about you and your health and fitness.' We all had a great respect for him and I think that worked both ways. He was always there for you with the Doc.

All the players took to John straight away and as time went by his disability was completely forgotten, apart from when he ran on to the pitch! I remember a game away at Wrexham, I had gone down injured and when John finally got to me, I smiled and said, 'F*****g hell John, hurry up, we are getting beat!' We both laughed, until I looked down and saw a hole in my knee!

One of my main strengths as a goalkeeper was bravery, which meant I got to spend a lot of time with John as he would regularly be patching me up. However, one particular injury had me wondering if I would survive. During a match away at Cambridge United, I was involved in an horrific impact with centre-forward George Reilly as he caught me high on the chest. I couldn't breathe and everyone around me started to panic as they realised the seriousness of the situation. John's quick thinking and expertise quickly stabilised my condition and to this day without him I honestly think I might not be here.

Another occasion I have to thank John for is helping me to recover from a serious neck injury. He managed to get me an appointment with a top neurosurgeon called Mr Hardy at Addenbrooke's Hospital in Cambridge. After undergoing various tests Mr Hardy diagnosed the injury and I had to undergo a long operation and stay in hospital for three weeks. As usual John watched the operation and would then regularly make a three-hour trip to monitor my progress. After leaving hospital, I still knew I was faced with a difficult rehabilitation period but with John's expertise, encouragement and professionalism I went on to play for another six or seven years.

He was an integral part of a well-oiled machine which included the manager, coaches, doctor, kit man, bus driver and many more. We all shared a close professional relationship which made the club a great place to be.

For all of the Luton Town players who haven't had this chance to contribute to this book, I will speak on their behalf and say, as a professional and also a personal friend, thank you, John, for all of your dedication to us as players and we are eternally grateful to have had a physiotherapist of such outstanding ability.

* * *

Kirk Stephens – Luton Town 1978–84

What can I say about John Sheridan that hasn't already been said? Everybody took to him straight away when he joined the club in the summer of 1979; even though he had a limp it was never an issue for the lads and in fact it made him even more special. He did his job brilliantly and coped with his disability fantastically well and we laughed with him about it. John would never belittle anybody and always had time for everybody. If you ever needed someone to speak to, he would always be there with an ear to offload your problems.

John as a physio learnt his trade in non-league and when he first made the big jump into the world of professional football he was understandably a little bit reserved, but he quickly came out of his shell and certainly gave as good as he got and was always a pleasure to be around.

One funny story that springs to mind involving John was an incident that happened in the build-up to a Saturday game against West Brom. In the week before the match, Pleaty gave us the Wednesday off. As I still ran a construction company in the Midlands, I took any opportunity to return home to help out, whether it be in the office or out on the sites. This particular Wednesday I was working on site at a factory and fell off the roof and landed on both feet on to a load of rubble, but within minutes both ankles had ballooned up. My first thought was, 'Oh shit, I'm in trouble now.' I still wanted to play on the Saturday so the next day I hobbled to the ground for training and came up with a story about having a puncture on the journey in and hurting my ankle on the brace as it slipped off the wheel nut. Even though both ankles were as bad as each other, I could only show John one of them. As I got on the bench for treatment, John took one look at my right ankle and immediately said, 'Kirk, this looks like window cleaner's ankle, it happens when somebody falls off a ladder or from a great height.'

He worked on that ankle all day and by the time I headed home it had improved immensely but my left ankle was still killing me. The next morning, I reported for treatment again and after John had looked after all of the other players I jumped on to the couch and this time took my left sock off. I said, 'John, unfortunately my ankle has come up again mate.' He started treating my left ankle and I could see him looking at me knowing something wasn't quite right. He then said, 'Kirk, I didn't treat that ankle yesterday, get your other sock off!' He asked how I'd done it so I replied, 'Well, it's window cleaner's ankle! I am desperate to play on Saturday and understand you are going to have to tell the gaffer but please give me any treatment you can.' He reassuringly said, 'Come on Kirk, let's see if we can get you fit.' He worked on me all day Friday and then early Saturday morning. After a late fitness test, I was miraculously passed fit and took my place in the starting 11 and managed to play 90 minutes. If the gaffer had found out he would have definitely fined me and left me out of the side but John being John didn't tell him and it remained our secret.

To this day I love the sound of his voice; it is a real calming voice that always fills you with confidence. He was loved by everybody at the club, still is, and whenever the players from that era reminisce about those brilliant days, John always springs to mind. Those days at Luton Town were the best of my life because of the people I was surrounded by, such as John, David Coates, the gaffer Pleaty and the rest of the squad.

I am so pleased John went on to have a great career in football and there is no bigger compliment than when your gaffer takes you to one of the biggest clubs in the country.

John was a players' man; he respected the lads so much and they all held him in the highest regard. I love him to bits and can't wait to see him again.

* * *

Steve Robinson – Tottenham Hotspur 1991–94; Luton Town 2002–08

I have known John for over 30 years, first meeting him as physio of Spurs when I was a 15-year-old from Belfast trying to make my way in the game. The bond we struck up straight away has stayed like that throughout the years, and not only with myself but also my family.

I had a career-threatening injury at the time and the quality of care and advice given to me by John, and most importantly how he treated me as a person, made me feel as though I was just as important as any first-team player to him. For a young, homesick boy with a career in the balance, the way John treated myself and my family and how positive he was in getting me back to playing and believing I could overcome the injury was something I will never forget.

Throughout the years I have always turned to John at the first sign of injury. He must have dreaded seeing my calls but nothing was ever too much trouble for him.

John was never flustered and had a calm, assured way about him. We had plenty of laughs along the way.

Over the years we have stayed in touch and followed each other's careers and when I signed for Luton in 2002 John was again the first person my family turned to.

Since I have been involved in football management, John and his family have remained my friends throughout and are always the first with a 'well done' or a message of support.

It is rare to meet genuine people in football but I managed to play nearly 500 games in my career and I truly believe that without John's support and quality of care I would not have even got close to that or even played at all.

I will be forever in debt to you and will always class you as a true friend.

* * *

Rob Johnson MCSP and SRP – Luton Town player and elite physiotherapist

In 1995 David Dandy published a paper that confirmed the success of an operation to replace the ruptured anterior cruciate ligament (ACL) and re-established the stability of the knee. This paper tracked patients who had the surgery between 1981 and 1984, reporting on their continued ability to lead normal lives, including several footballers that had returned to the elite level.

I was one of that group having ruptured my right ACL in August 1982 and my left one in December 1983. When I finally resumed playing in the summer of 1985, I had become the first player to play in the First Division to have recovered from two ruptured ACLs, and in the process lost three years of my life to four surgeries and months of rehabilitation.

Remarkably and somewhat perplexingly, the technique Dandy employed was not some new innovation using revolutionary material or ideas. Instead it was based largely on a procedure developed by a surgeon called Groves in 1920. With some adaptations copied from Campbell in 1964 and MacIntosh in 1972, Dandy had produced an operation that could tolerate the stresses and strains of sport at the highest level, something that had hitherto been almost impossible. It was somewhat perplexing because the method had been lost or ignored by many surgeons for so long. While the reasons for this interlude can only be speculated upon, what is certain is that in that period of time the dreams, careers and lives of so many footballers were ripped apart by this injury.

The fact that I was able to return to the First Division twice is an obvious testament to the excellence of the surgery. However, while the surgeon could reference various colleagues who had helped in this major leap forward, my physiotherapist, who would guide, push and care for me over nine months of gruelling rehabilitation, twice in three years, would find little in the literature to underpin the path we would need to take.

Indeed, it is made all the more astonishing when you consider John's daily responsibilities for 40 full-time professional footballers as well as the care for another long-term injured player in Mike Saxby, all in the season that saw Luton survive relegation by defeating Manchester City in the very last game at Maine Road. You may begin to understand the enormity of his achievement.

Physiotherapists in those days had an almost guru-like status among the players. It was expected that the physiotherapist would not only be able to diagnose every injury himself, but could treat, rehabilitate and give an exact date for a return to full fitness. This belief was often confirmed for the players at least when they were sent for a specialist consultation and returned more disappointed than enlightened. Their time, they thought, had been wasted due to the lack of sports medicine expertise at that time. In this situation it is easy to fall into a trap of believing the status so readily bestowed on you by these returning players and resorting to your own trusted methods to treat an unknown injury.

In this febrile environment John Sheridan was always the calmest man around; nothing seemed to fluster him and he would always be the most positive and optimistic in any given situation. He had the total trust of the manager and the players were only too aware that his focus was always on their health and wellbeing. Furthermore, he never fell into the guru trap; his way was built on solid evidence and he always sought the best advice he could when dealing with the unknown. For this, I will always be truly grateful.

It is hard to explain now what John was faced with as even gaining a clear diagnosis was far from straightforward. There were no scans or sports medicine expertise available. Those things simply didn't exist. The only investigation open to us was an x-ray which has little value in detecting soft tissue injuries and John was left to decide if it was worthwhile seeking a specialist's opinion, and if so who. These were all decisions for John to make and thankfully he made the right one. We went to see Mr Dandy who, after listening intently to what I had to say in relation to how I got injured, quickly did three tests that he said confirmed that my medial collateral ligament was intact, but that I had ruptured my ACL and although I could try and play again, I may find it difficult. In that case he would operate and I would be out for a minimum of six months. I listened to this two-minute discourse but understood very little of what had just been said; it would become clearer in time.

Of course, today's players do not even consider trying to play following this diagnosis, but in 1982 every option had to be explored and so I tried to strengthen my knee enough to train and hopefully play again. At this stage I was very optimistic as I had no idea what I was up against. But a few weeks and three collapsing episodes later it was clear that surgery was my only option.

Following the operation, I was on crutches for two months and my leg was bent to about 40 degrees; it would take six long months to get it fully straight and, in this time, I followed John's decrees unquestioningly. When I began my rehabilitation in earnest, I would be given a programme that was biased in favour of the hamstring and calf muscles over the quadriceps muscles. John explained that this would protect the graft while at the same time increase both my strength and range of movement. Many of these exercises would be progressed from two legs to one leg with balance and dynamic movement to follow. John said I could do as many as I wanted to because the graft would come to no harm. So I built up my strength and increased my range of movement by doing 1,000 reps a day. My days were typically long and included cycling, swimming and later running and ball work. John's genius was to provide a programme that a young, competitive and hungry athlete could eat up day after day while being perfectly safe. The knee felt great after each session – no swelling, no pain and I could repeat this feat day after day.

John never doubted for one second what we were doing; his faith in me and the programme never wavered.

John single-handedly accomplished for me something that today requires a large multi-disciplinary team (MDT) of health and fitness professionals to undertake. His accomplishment is perhaps best understood and appreciated when you compare the two examples. The first is how present-day footballers are managed when they sustain the same injury, and the second is how in the past it could all so easily have gone wrong.

Today the surgery has been developed and alongside it the rehabilitation process. There still remains nine months of intense work guided by many of the same principles laid down by John for me in the 1980s. But there the similarities end. In today's football clubs, the players are surrounded by sports medicine expertise and rigid protocols that are carried out by members of the MDT. From the first minute the injury is suspected a diagnosis will be confirmed by MRI followed by the full weight of the MDT swinging into action. This is a large team comprising typically a sports physician or doctor, several physiotherapists, strength and conditioning coaches, nutritionists, psychologists, physiologists and visual analysts. They work closely together and separately, with different specialisms taking the lead in the rehabilitation process at different times. World-leading surgeons and radiologists will feed into the team usually at the direction of the sports physician.

The long period of time during rehabilitation will mean the player has reduced and altered mental and physical activity compared to his normal routine and the psychologist and nutritionist will closely monitor this. The physiotherapy team will set the early rehabilitation programme feeding into strength and condition coaches the boundaries of daily and weekly activity. As the rehabilitation progresses, data from jump, hop and running tests taken before the player was injured will be used to compare to his present state, while visual analysis will compare his present movement during running and later football activity with previous data from games and training sessions.

This support envelops the player in a protective bubble, reducing the risk of potential physical or mental problems during the long rehabilitation period. It also acts to support individual therapists, so that their role is never overwhelming, with responsibility and pressure shared throughout.

The risk of mistakes and a breakdown in either relationships within the team or the trust of the player is minimised. The management of risk is always at the forefront of the collective team's mind. The football manager is kept up to speed with all developments, and the scheduled return to training and playing is factored in with all the team members contributing to the plan. In this way the load is shared and the risk is minimised.

The management of risk is always made harder by increased workloads and the unmitigated build-up of pressure that can so easily occur in an environment that existed in 1980s football. That my story could have finished so differently can be illustrated by a player who like me sustained this dreadful injury in those uncertain times. I had played against him and have spoken to him briefly since about his experiences. The story of Paul Lake is one that highlights how even the best and brightest among us can have their futures ruined.

Paul, unfortunately, in 1990 – some eight years after my first injury – suffered an ACL rupture in what seemed to the commentator on the television 'a quite innocuous challenge'. Paul, like me, had an x-ray which showed no bone damage, but then unlike me no further investigations or opinions were sought and he was rehabilitated back to football not knowing that he had ruptured his ACL. What followed is documented extensively in his book *I'm Not Really Here*. To date he has had 15 operations and has suffered all kinds of physical and mental health problems. I met Paul long after we finished playing and both of us were qualified physiotherapists so our shared history of football, ACL injuries, operations, rehabilitation and physiotherapy gave us plenty to talk about. His knee would not allow him to pursue an active life as a physiotherapist and he now works as an ambassador at Manchester City.

My story could so easily have finished so differently.

Many of my reflections of John's work have come about since I became a physiotherapist. I too have worked at the highest levels in sport and understand the pressures that are daily companions and the need to be always one step ahead in any given situation. This includes referring to specialists and providing options to athletes and coaches and communicating to all clearly what our shared outcomes should be. Working as part of a large team can bring its own pressures but ultimately it leads to clearer planning, time for reflection and easier adaptation for challenging situations. We often need time just to think and this can be difficult in the environment that is elite sport.

I am now 59 years old. I play football daily with my seven-year-old son and run and train as much as time and family allow. But for the 8in scars on both my knees you would be hard-pressed to know I had anything done. They don't swell, I have no pain and I have full range of motion. My manager David Pleat is someone I have huge respect and admiration for. I played and worked for him at Luton, Leicester and Sheffield Wednesday. His wisdom, passion and for me compassion made him the best manager in the country during the 1980s and early '90s. His eye for a player was unrivalled with many astute signings and he looked to play the kind of football we are now witnessing today. One of his very best signings was a man with a limp who didn't move very well and was softly spoken in company and shied away from the limelight. In his quiet moments you could catch him smoking his pipe at the end of the tunnel, reflecting on the day's events and planning for the next. In this way he looked after us all and taught me so much into the bargain. This man inspired me to take up physiotherapy because of his brilliance and his dedication, but most of all because he cared.

One thing I will always remember is when John picked me up after my first operation in Cambridge and drove me home to my mum in our little council flat in Bedford. He was pretty weary from his day at work but took on the responsibility of picking me up after such an awful operation. My mum was a little shocked by my appearance as I had lost over a stone in five days at the hospital and as I sat down, he looked at me and my mum and saw our need for reassurance, even though we said nothing. Rather than rushing out to get home, he sat down and had a cup of tea with us, spending 45 minutes chatting, smiling and just being there. He knew we needed comforting.

What a man!

* * *

Alan Smith – Sheffield Wednesday and England physiotherapist
I feel it is an honour and privilege to be asked to contribute to John's book.

I remember all those years ago when we first met at Lilleshall on a Football Association medical course and shared a room together. I think we got on right from the start because we were of the same mind, both very passionate about what we were aiming for and knew that only hard work would achieve what we wanted to do. The staff on the course were Paddy Armour (senior lecturer), Geoff Ladley (Leeds United), John McVey

(Leicester City) and Jimmy Headridge (Middlesbrough), who were all brilliant. I remember how we were both in our element to be with these football people and couldn't get enough of what they were teaching. We were like sponges. We passed the first year and attended for the next two consecutive years. Each time we were room-mates and as such, our friendship grew.

As the years went by, we kept in touch with each other while moving from club to club and I always followed John's career with great interest. I can truly say that his ability as a physiotherapist is outstanding. Having achieved what he has in his career, working at the top level of football with Tottenham Hotspur, helping the club win the FA Cup in 1991, working with one of the greatest managers in Terry Venables and seeing how he helped one of the world's most famous footballers, namely Paul Gascoigne, recover from a very serious knee injury, deserves so much credit.

It is of no surprise to me that John has had such a great career because of his love for his job and his passion for learning. He is one of the nicest and most pleasant people anyone could meet, and this, along with his very high standards both personally and professionally, go hand in hand with his success.

It has been a great pleasure to have had John as a friend for all these years.

* * *

Trevor Hartley – first-team coach, Luton Town and Tottenham Hotspur

I have known John since June 1980 when I was appointed as a coach at Luton Town and John was the club's physiotherapist.

I was asked once about my thoughts on his 'disability'. I really had to think hard about this as I only ever saw John as a very competent physio. Yes, John has a limp which possibly restricted his movement on the pitch but didn't alter the fact that he evaluated the injured player quickly to decide whether he could carry on playing or he should leave the field of play.

John always had the total respect of all players, staff and especially the club doctors for his hard work and immense knowledge in his field of work. They knew he would go the extra mile, even carrying out further treatment at his own practice and in his own time.

John had a very successful career in football, both at Luton and then Tottenham Hotspur with manager David Pleat, and his reputation was such that when new manager Terry Venables came on board, he was retained in his position.

John became even more recognised within the football fraternity when his expertise was instrumental in the full recovery of a very serious injury to Paul Gascoigne.

Many other players will agree that they have John to thank for prompt decisions he made for them during their playing careers and not one of those players would have given John's 'disability' a second thought.

So, for me personally, as an ex-work colleague and especially as a friend, I have never felt the need to dwell on John's injury. To me it was all about his sheer professionalism, knowledge, enthusiasm and kindness throughout.

Acknowledgements

I WOULD like to thank all the people who agreed to make contributions to this book. Their kind words were extremely humbling and without doubt I have been very privileged to have worked for two of the best clubs in the world in Luton Town and Tottenham Hotspur. A big thank you must go to the players, medical staff, managers, coaches and kit men for all of the help and support I was kindly given. A special thank you must go to the fans of these two great clubs as whenever I ran on to the pitch, I always felt your support and loyalty.

I will be forever grateful to all of the surgeons who allowed me into their operating theatres to watch them at work. My knowledge of living anatomy was enhanced in a way that I could only have dreamed about. Their cooperation made it much easier for me to do my job.

I owe a debt of gratitude to three men who had a profound effect on my life. The first is Pete Wyder, who was my manager at Taverners all of those years ago. He supported me in so many ways and encouraged me to be the best physio I possibly could be. The second person is David Pleat, who took a calculated risk when he employed me at Luton Town in 1979. He is a great man who had the utmost faith in me as a person and my ability to do the job. The third person is Terry Venables, who allowed me the chance to carry on working at Tottenham and complete a treasured part of my career at such a great club. Without doubt it was a privilege to work for these fine managers. My footballing story would not be complete without thanking the non-league clubs that I served for a number of years, which include Taverners, Vauxhall Motors and Tring Town. This time of my life allowed me to learn my craft at a good level.

A big thank you must go to David Pleat and Gary Mabbutt for taking the time to write the forewords for this book.

This book wouldn't have seen the light of day without the following people: my youngest son Paul for writing the story of my life and encouraging me to keep putting my memories on to paper; Luton Town historian Roger Wash and Hatters Heritage for helping me with information from that era; the use of Gareth Owen's photo collection; Pitch Publishing for their belief and expertise in allowing me to realise my dream of putting my life story into print. Thank you to all of you.

A special thank you must go to Gavin Blackwell, who has helped in so many ways. He is not only a talented physio but also an encyclopaedia on the medical side of football. Over the last 34 years he has gained a vast amount of knowledge and experience within professional football at Wolverhampton Wanderers' academy and through semi-professional football. In 2010 he was presented with the prestigious Football Medicine and Performance Association 21 Club award, which recognises medical practitioners who have worked in professional football for 21 years.

Having overseen a mammoth 1,800 games over three decades in the dugout, he has an excellent knowledge on all aspects of football medicine with multiple qualifications at FIFA, UEFA and Football Association levels.

I have to thank all of my lovely family for their love and support. My beautiful wife Betty has always been my rock. My children Debbie, Andy and Paul, despite me having to make sacrifices during their childhood, have always supported me. I am so proud of them all and who they have grown in to. They have all made fantastic choices in their life and now have lovely families of their own in Tracy, Jayne, Colin, Louise (RIP) and my grandchildren Jake, Sam, Lucy and Edward, who were the reason for writing this book.

To my mum and dad for all of their love and my beloved sisters Anne (RIP) and Pat and their fantastic husbands John (RIP) and Jim, with whom we have always shared a close and loving relationship. I would also like to thank my two brothers, Tommy (RIP) and Tony, and their wives Josie and Marie for their love and support throughout the difficult times I experienced during my childhood.

Lastly, my story wouldn't have been told if it wasn't for the care and attention of the staff at the Luton and Dunstable Hospital who saved my life all those years ago, and thank you also to the Royal National Orthopaedic Hospital for giving me a life after my accident.

A portion of any profits from this book will be donated to charity. One recipient will be the Pancreatic Cancer Research Fund in memory of my niece Nicki, a very caring, talented physiotherapist, who is very sadly missed.

Also available at all good book stores

9781785316470

9781785313929

9781785315466

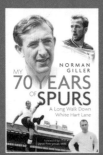

9781785318894

9781908051776

9781785313264

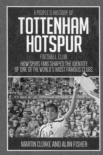

9781785311888

9781785315985

9781905411863